The Innovator

Interview with John Bailey

The Aiki Dialogues - N. 12

The Innovator - Interview with John Bailey

Simone Chierchini

Copyright © 2022 Aikido Italia Network Publishing

First edition

Publisher: Aikido Italia Network Publishing
Tavanaghmore, Foxford, Co. Mayo, Ireland
(00353) 083- 8713927
https://aikidoitalianetworkpublishing.com

Front and Back Cover Photos © John Bailey

Cover and layout design by Simone Chierchini

Some of the images utilized in this book were found online. Despite our best efforts, we could not locate the correct copyright holder. No challenge to copyright is intended

No part of this book can be reproduced or used in any form or by any means without prior written permission of the publisher

ISBN: 9798803139584

Imprint: Independently published on Amazon KDP

Simone Chierchini

The Innovator
Interview with John Bailey

Aikido Italia Network Publishing

AIKIDO ITALIA NETWORK
Publishing

Table of Contents

Biographical Notes	7
Introduction	9
The Martial Art's Path	13
The Struggle to Learn in the Aiki Community	19
Alternative Teaching Methods	23
Getting Rid of the Unnecessary Super-structure	27
The Domain of Technique Collectors	33
A Verifiable Approach	41
Bones Can Snap	47
Not Enough Time	51
The Naming Convention Issue in Aikido	55
Generalisation vs Specification	63
The Way of Uke	67
How to Develop an Aiki Body	71
Is Cross Training a Bad Word?	75
To Compete or not To Compete?	79
Supplement 1: Look Into the Mirror	84
Supplement 2: Cultural Conundrum	92

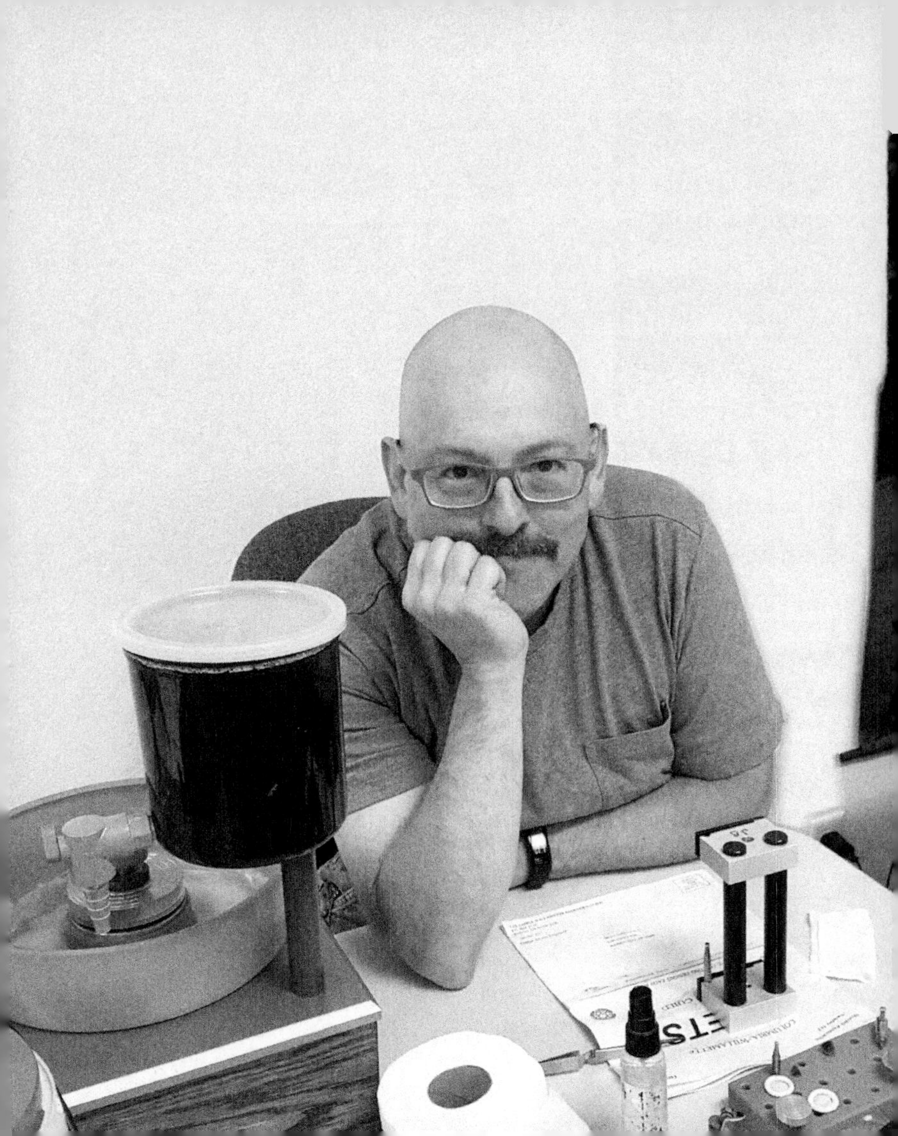

Biographical Notes

John Bailey studied Aikido under Tony Graziano and Tom Walker.

He is a graduate of Executive Security International and has an extensive background in security and investigations, having worked as a bouncer, security officer, bodyguard, undercover operative and tactical instructor.

He was a practical firearms competitor and instructor and has provided tactical training for law enforcement and private security agencies in Florida, Colorado, California and Oregon. He's a life-long student of violence, the behavioural factors and practical implications of it.

He is a certified clinical hypnotist, and co-creator of the Motivational Literacy system of self-development, innovating anger management strategies.

He's presently focused on the navigation of crisis periods, and creating fulfilment through life design.

John has studied Aikido for four decades, the past two of which have been dedicated to exploring better ways to train and to teach the art in a quickly changing world.

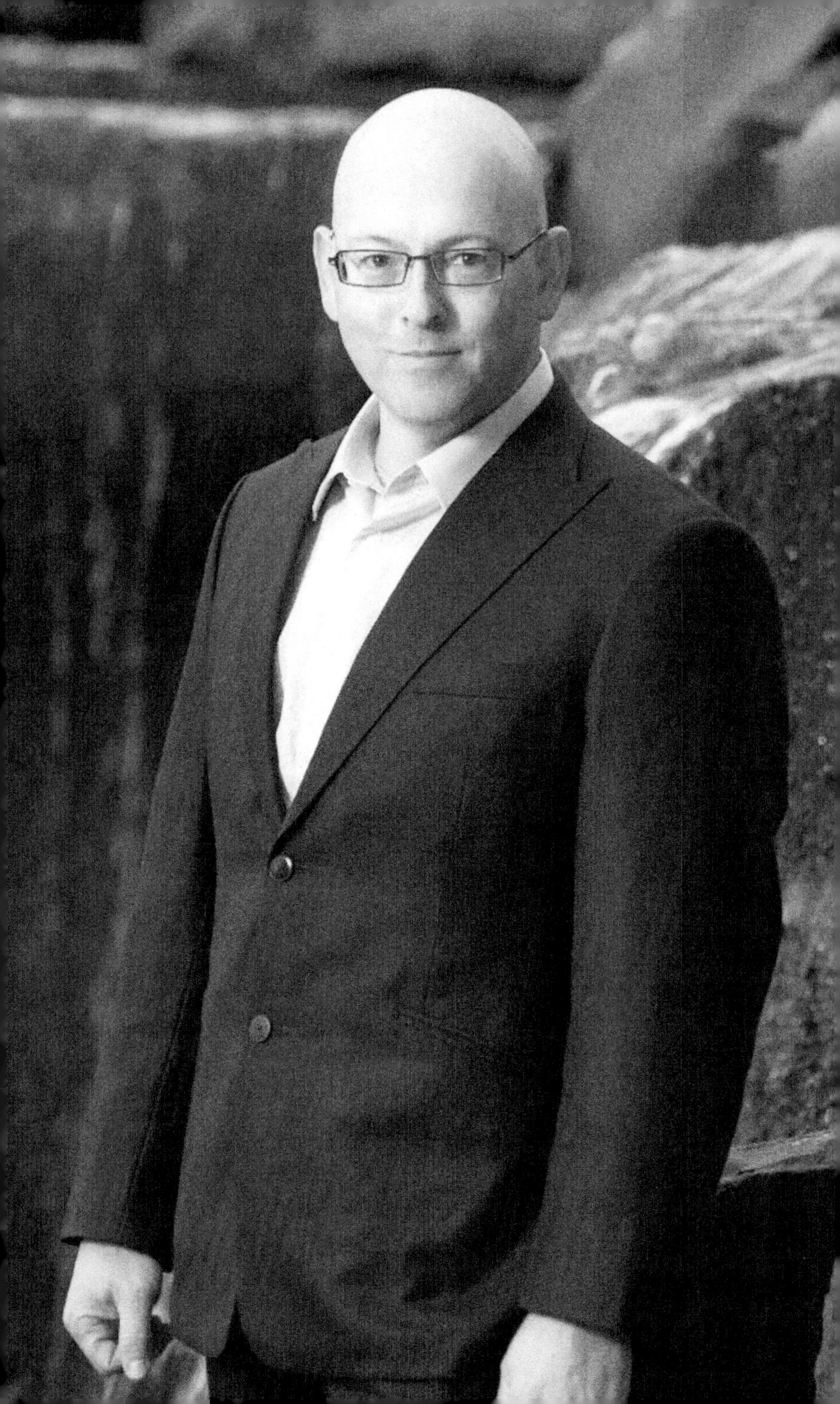

Introduction

"The weak can never forgive.
Forgiveness is the attribute of the strong"
(Mahatma Gandhi)

A few weeks ago, by a mere strike of luck, I managed to get my hands on "The Magic of Aikido – A Thesis on Progressive Aikido Training Methods". It is a work that was produced by John Bailey in 2000 in quite an arcane format – a pdf e-book saved as an ISO file burnable to a CD. The book is not currently available to the general public.

Bailey's work references the contributions of Bruce K. Siddle – a law enforcement veteran specialising in training and survival human factors and the founder of PPCT Management Systems – and his documentation of factors like reaction times and how those relate to the size/length of cognitive programs. It talks specifically about how Aikido, in particular, suffers from performance problems, especially in younger (newer) students, owing to the "code-bloat" of the conventional naming conventions.

Bailey tells how along his Aikido travels, he attended a seminar where no talking was allowed. He saw instructors teaching footwork that was hidden by their hakama. Those training methods left him puzzled. Reading and re-reading the standard requirements for various grade promotions, he could find neither real-world relevance nor any logical pattern to them.

This is the reason why he began to question traditional teaching practices, comparing them to modern sports training technology. After reading Bruce Siddle's studies on performance under stress, he started experimenting with new training methods, changing students' habits — then testing student reaction times and performance. He rewrote grade requirements based on a logical pattern and real-world relevance.

The Magic of Aikido is based on hard science, and measurable outcomes. It lays out the state of strategies that John Bailey formulated to teach Aikido, with specific attention towards accelerating performance, 20 years ago, when his work was first published. Since then, this exploration has come a long way, as John has explained to me in the informal discussion that we are now happy to share with you.

The Magic of Aikido

A THESIS ON PROGRESSIVE AIKIDO TRAINING METHODS BY JOHN BAILEY

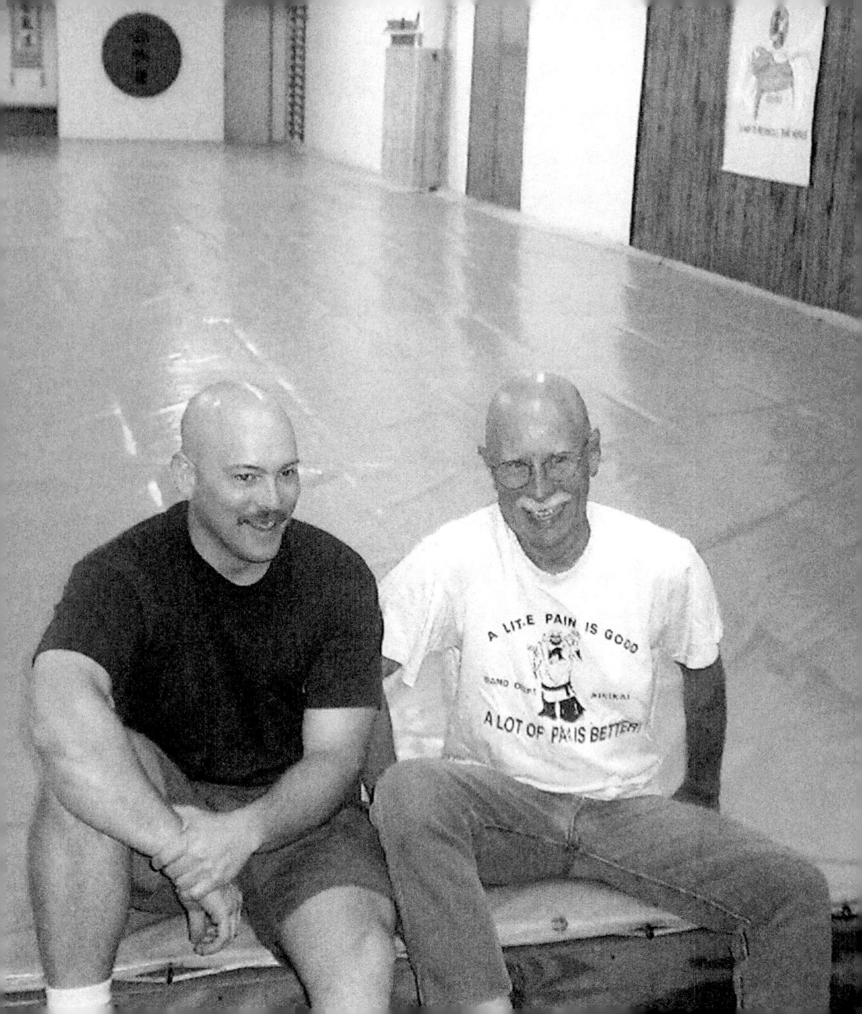
PAIN IS GOOD
IS BETTER

The Martial Art's Path

"Can you tell us a bit about your path in martial arts? How, when and why did you get attracted to them?"

"When I was a small child, due to illness I missed so much of first grade that I had to repeat it. I was a smaller boy, both sickly and bookish. One might expect I was bullied a bit during early elementary school years. One of the natural reactions to such early life experience is overcompensation.
"In the Summer between 4th and 5th grades, I took a self defense class, hoping the next school year would be less troublesome. That instructor was only in his teens, and was really excellent, and encouraging toward further exploration. The bullying reduced significantly, and I also started taking a hard style of Japanese Karate. I didn't really excel, but did greatly enjoy it. In high school my practice dropped-off for a few years.
"After leaving school, I wandered into an Aikido *dojo*, and thought 'this stuff is nonsense - with all this turning around in circles - that's not fighting'. I expressed that sentiment to the instructor after the class, and was treated to a 30-40 minute long explanation by Tom Walker and Grady Lane (who is now shihan, and who has been my friend and one of my *sensei* since that time). Their explanation was

sensible, and inspired me to explore Aikido hands-on. I was at that time, also beginning to work as a bouncer in night clubs…

"From there, I entered the dojo of Tony Graziano - a man far larger than life. He was a power-lifting competitor. If memory serves, he was *sandan* in Shotokan Karate, and was on the SWAT team. He looked and moved like a tiger on the prowl - and had the same explosive quality when he did anything. He used to talk about how his meeting Tom Walker inspired him to take off his Shotokan black belt and put on an Aikido white belt. He did *tanto dori* with a sharpened bayonet - at 100% speed. You'd attack him full-speed, and next thing you were disconnected from Mother Earth and the lights were spinning past. You knew there was his flesh, your flesh, and the mats you didn't want to cut - and somewhere in that storm was that damn big sharp knife…

"Neither he, nor *uke*, nor the mats ever got cut. Both uke and knife were always positively controlled. He was just like that. He practised and taught Iaido – always with sharp, live blades. This was my first Aikido sensei, and role model when I was maybe 19 years old.

"After some years, I began to train mostly in Tom Walker's *dojo*. All dojo have a culture – made up from the people and traditions they embrace. They're all unique, and we may not really think about judging them when we're just students. As a young man I was looking to the Sensei and advanced students (mostly men in their 30's to 50's) as models and mentors.

"We often don't realise the gifts and privileges of our circumstances until we look back on them with the perspective of years and experience. The dojo I stumbled into at 19 was a more-than-special environment. The location was Titusville, Florida – which is straight across the lagoon from Kennedy Space Center (one block out the back door of the dojo was the shore line – and a great seat for watching

Tom "Doc" Walker

launches). *Dojo Cho* was Tom 'Doc' Walker. He was called 'Doc' because he was a dentist. He was a vibrantly-energetic polymath, who obsessively wrote poetry, tended *bonsai* trees, studied *ikebana*, and designed and built custom knives. He read voraciously, and could quote a very broad range of authors on many topics. So, there's a role model. And, that alone would have been something. But, Doc was just the centre of gravity.

"The dojo included a man named Alan Drysdale, who was a PhD involved in designing life support systems for the space program. He was about a *yondan* at that time. And, I think Steve House was about the same rank. He was on the local SWAT team. Dr. Paul Buchanan was director of biomedical research at NASA Kennedy Space Center – and about a *nidan* at that time. Paul's wife Anne was, I think, a PhD – and I think nidan. There was a guy named Chuck Gould, who was I think, nidan, and I believe a combat veteran. And, there was a highly-decorated Army Ranger combat veteran named Howell Hilton, who was, I think, nidan at that time, and who would become a close friend for around 40 years until his passing just last year.

"So, we get some idea of the uniquely rich, and enriching environment in which my Aikido career sprouted. We can read into the kinds of minds and attitudes I was surrounded by – in terms of study, evaluation, and adaptation of technique. All the higher-ups were highly-educated: they knew anatomy, biology, psychology. And many had hands-on experience in combat – or depended on their Aikido daily, literally for survival.

"In 1992, just months shy of when I was slated to test for *shodan*, I moved to Oregon. There was no dojo within 100 miles. The nearest one was over a mountain pass that was treacherous with snow in the winter. I drove over to train with Darrell Bluhm sensei (now also shihan) on occasion, but found it necessary to start teaching in order to practise more than once per week.

"The people who showed up mostly had other martial arts experience. And, many of them resembled refrigerators – or tractors – in their size and strength. I had Judo players, college-level wrestlers. And, they wanted to 'see if Aikido works'. I trained THE BASICS, and often with stronger, and resistive people. I met and cross-trained with some practitioners of Filipino Martial Arts.

"That's where I learned drills that offer what I call 'intermediate contrivance' - and which I've adapted to Aikido training. From FMA edged weapon practice, I also got an entirely different perspective on all the *kata dori* practice we do in Aikido: 100% of those methods are really *tanto dori* - where *nage* is the one with the tanto. That kind of epiphany – and practice derived from it – is a logical direction to go, given my Aikido roots…"

With "Doc" Walker and Barry "Dart" Richardson

Kazuo Chiba

The Struggle to Learn in the Aiki Community

"What did you not like about the way you were seeing Aikido being taught?"

"I'm not sure I would say I did 'not like' the ways Aikido was taught. Any training has merits of some kind. And, excepting people who were clearly abusive to students, I've always found things to like and enjoy – and useful take-aways.

"I particularly enjoyed training with Darrell Bluhm sensei – and with Chiba shihan. I never had any reservation about giving myself fully to an attack with Bluhm sensei – never concerned for my well being. His techniques were always powerful; always smooth; always facilitated *ukemi*.

"There's a particularly beautiful experience of taking ukemi behind a 100% committed attack – with someone whose Aikido has those qualities. I've been privileged to have such magical moments with three of the men I've called Sensei. The moment of self-abandonment – into a fully-blended Aikido – and a safe and comfortable landing – is pure magic.

"My background – and much of my work still - contained 'hands-on-in-the-real-world'. It also contained

The Innovator

the need to help people progress rapidly. I also wanted to explore my own points of frustration, mainly that traditional Aikido practice range and stylised attacks were very unrealistic for actual encounters. And, this was one of the big challenges in translating dojo to street."

Darrell Bluhm

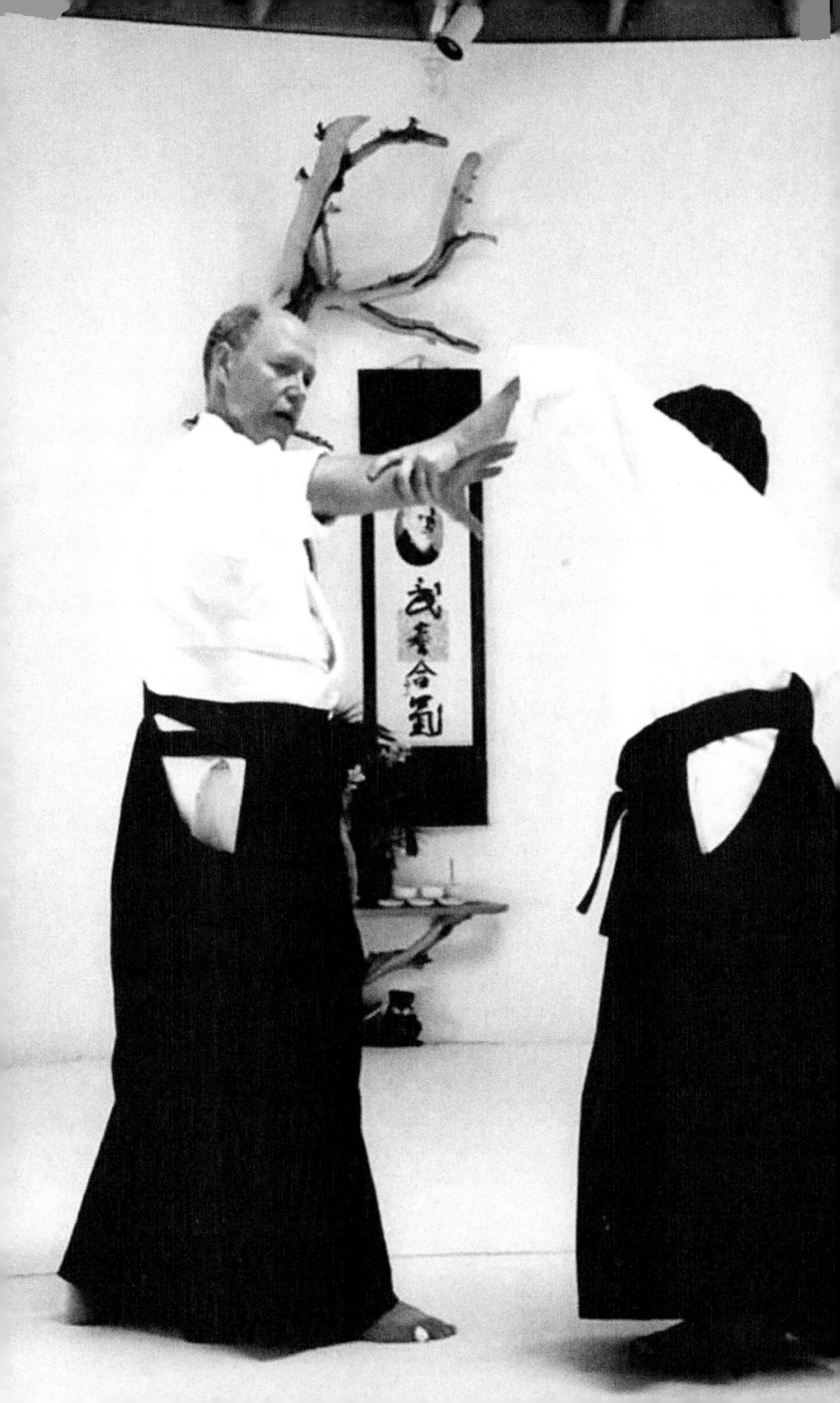
武産合氣

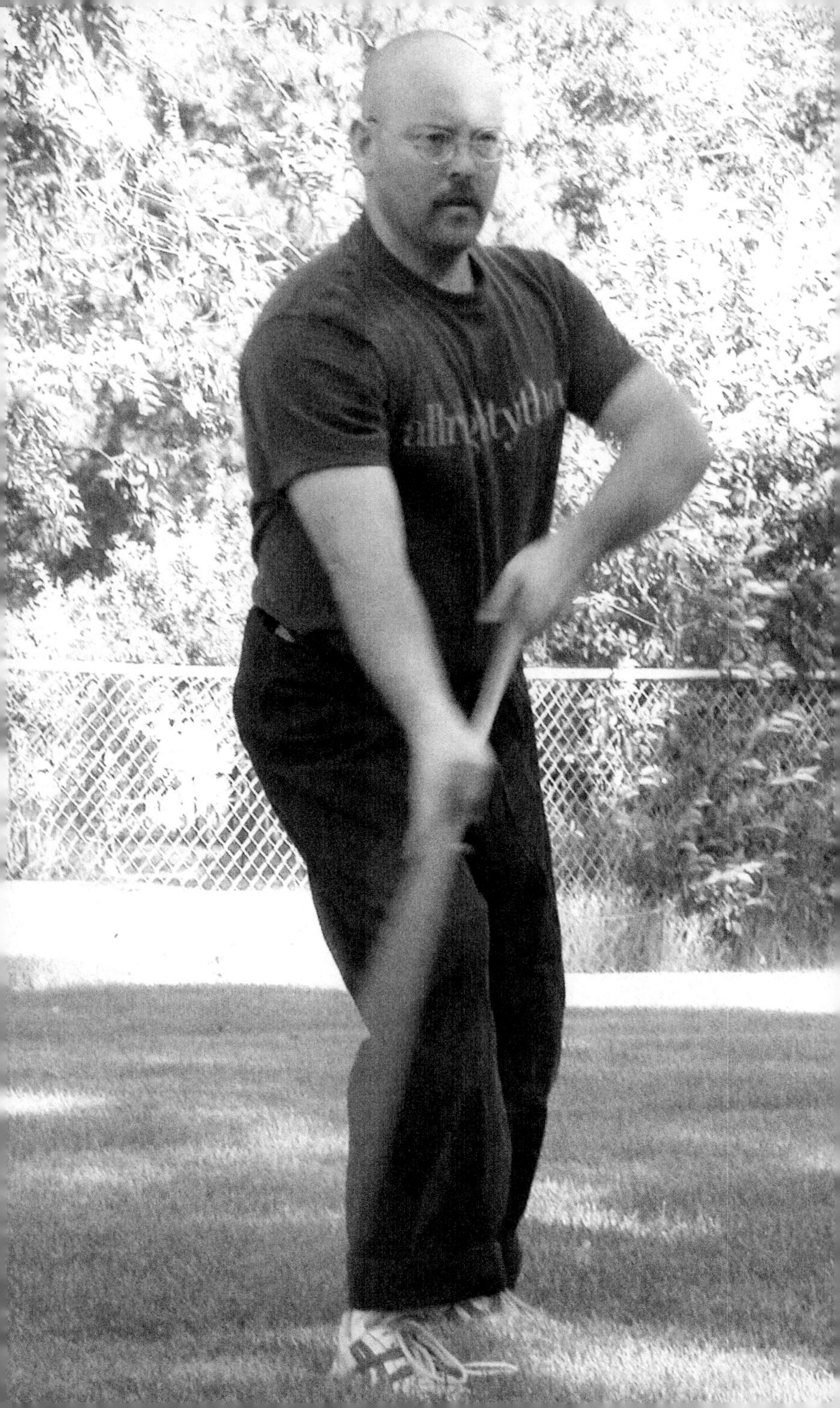

Alternative Teaching Methods

"How did your teaching interests take a course so different from what is considered standard or 'traditional' in the Aikido community?"

"If we parse the word 'teaching', it unpacks differently according to culture and background. Mine was with these American instructors with medicine, biology, engineering, military, weapon-craft backgrounds. The traditional Eastern approach that is somewhat 'you get what you are able to notice' seemed dishonest to me. If you're paying someone to teach you, then they should TEACH you – and in a way that moves you along.

"I had another motive in that I was isolated geographically, and if I wanted to throw someone in a certain way – or train at a certain level – it was most efficient for me to bring someone to that level rather than for me to travel. What I increasingly saw as an ethical issue aside, I needed my students to progress quickly – for my own interests.

"I had done tactical firearms training with John Farnham, and had been a competitive shooter. I knew the principles from reading authors like Bruce Siddle, and studying things like Hick's law of motor learning. I knew how to shorten reaction times. My wife has a master's degree in education. So I had access to 'best practices' in learning and conveying information. And, I had become a certified clinical hypnotist, learning a great deal about how information and reflexive responses pack into – and then unpack from – the neurology.

"I spent vast amounts of time studying what is Aikido, informationally, cognitively, neurologically – and asking one main question:

'If this were a body of information that I just had – and there were no established way of transmitting it – how would I create a way to install this set of knowledge and of responses to stimuli to other people?'

"So, trying to answer that question – to the best demonstrable outcome – has been my guiding question and principle for the past 25 years. And, this is the context for finding it strange to hold a seminar – and there's no talking allowed. Or, we're wearing *hakama* that hides our feet and hips. From whom are we hiding these things? Our paying students are the only people in the room…

"Reading and re-reading the standard requirements for various grade promotions, I don't find a logical or efficient taxonomy. I think this is due to the way most martial arts are cobbled from oral tradition – and senior instructors or founders label things they've discovered, or created on-the-fly. It's the nature of something that grows organically.

"When we look at modern sports training technology and things like studies on performance under stress, we can weigh the value of 'keeping tradition' against the value of upgrading an instructional program to best-known practices and performance science. I experimented with training methods, changed students' habits – then tested reaction times and performance. I rewrite grade requirements based on those experiments – on measured outcomes.

"I'm currently in the midst of what I think is the next generation of this development paradigm – with methods specifically about *randori*, integrated into teaching and practising with individual partners."

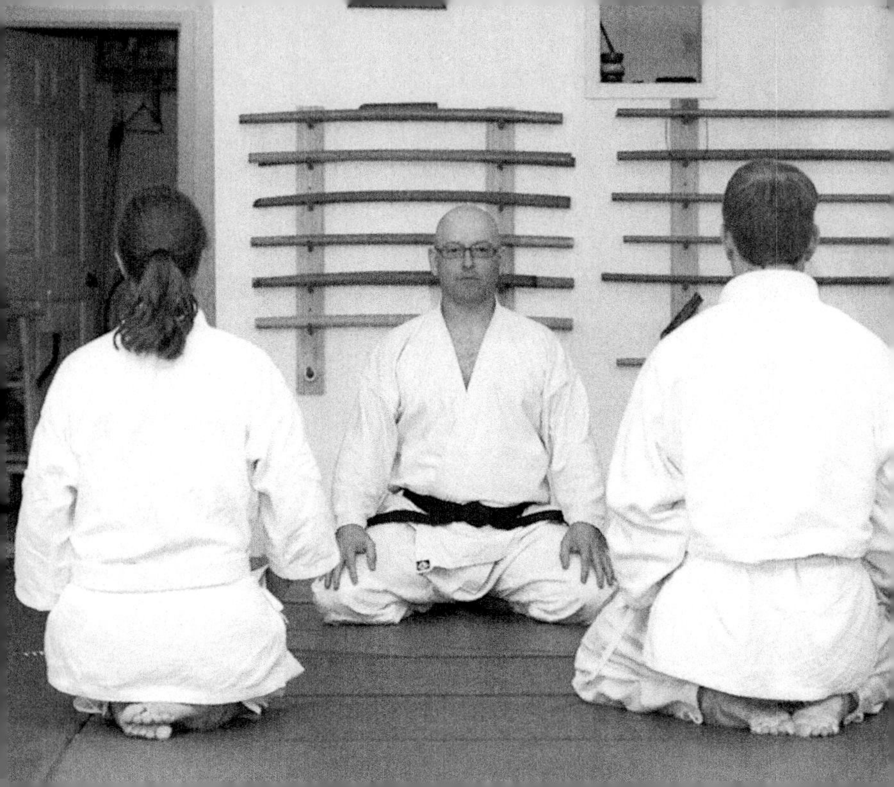

Getting Rid of the Unnecessary Super-structure

"In your book *The Magic of Aikido* you state the following: 'It is not necessary for Aikido training to be confusing, mysterious, or obscured by a costume. It is not necessary for Aikido to be learned more slowly than other arts. And, it is wrong for us to impose handicaps on our students in the name of tradition, costume, or *ki* magic. The paths of *Bushido* can be dangerous, and we are obliged to provide the best possible means in the shortest possible time – even if we must learn new methods and establish new traditions to do so'. Care to expand on this?"

"I think this is parsing the word 'teach'.

"People in the modern West understand 'sensei' as 'teacher'. And, when they sign up at a dojo, they understand they're 'purchasing lessons' or 'buying teaching'. So, there's some ethical consideration with regard to the transaction – according to the customer's understanding of what they're paying for.

"There's also the issue that teaching something is a distinct skill separate from doing that thing oneself. Not everyone who can do a thing – even at a high level – can impart their knowledge or install skills to another person, especially efficiently. For example, many coaches of titleholding boxers never themselves held titles.

"If the actual goal of teaching is transmission of a skill to others, then baseline competence to that goal requires having an understanding of the neurology and psychology of the skill itself, as well as the learning processes, and the factors that affect performance of the skill outside the classroom. There's a whole modern science around how humans learn – and best practices to facilitate both learning and performance – including performance under acute stress.

"Concealing key mechanics of a skill behind an almost literal curtain (hakama) is anti-teaching. It's effort counter to the stated intent – and to a transaction, where someone has purchased 'teaching'. The question I had to ask myself was whether the approach was dishonest (we didn't really intend to teach) or just less-than-competent at doing that.

"I felt compelled to ask that same question about every other aspect of the process. Language is the software of the human mind. We're using this odd language that adds a layer of complexity and confusion. The language we use is ambiguous: how many kinds of *kotegaeshi* are there? And, what one political organisation calls '*hiji kime*' another calls '*juji nage*'. I fly from Florida to attend a seminar in California - and part of my vocabulary stops working. Any software guy will tell you that's just 'bad coding'.

"The ways we conceptualise, store, and recall what we call 'Aikido' have a dramatic influence on the rate at which we can absorb it, and the effectiveness with which we perform it. Any *do* is at least in part about continuing to improve oneself by honing one's understanding and practices, indefinitely. This includes the teaching and empowering of students. And, I feel ethically obligated to do the best job I can in teaching, using demonstrated best practices.

"To that end, I feel obligated to some... housekeeping – of things that don't tangibly contribute to communicating, learning, and performing the physical art – and especially if they create drag on the system.

The Innovator

"A convoluted naming convention is mentally cluttering, and results in a massively bloated classification strategy: how many 'Aikido techniques' are there?

"The answer depends on how we define an 'Aikido technique'. The mechanics of kotegaeshi, for instance, are found in arts across Asia – and in systems that pre-date Aikido. So, independent of all other bits, do the mechanics specific to kotegaeshi constitute 'an Aikido technique'? I don't think so.

"The naming convention we see consistently used is structured [attack] – [termination], and sometimes qualified by an omote/ura designation, which indicates where the [termination] should take place, relative to uke.

"We get into simple math of reasonable permutations of [attack], times some permutations of [termination], times two (omote/ura) = some bloated number.

"But, how many different ways do we move to bypass the attack, to manipulate uke, and arrive at the omote or ura quasi-location at which we actually reverse the wrist? Let's for argument say there are about eight primary ways of moving and a couple of additional transitional movements for a ballpark of ten. So, take the already-bloated number and multiply by ten.

"That's what a student needs to recognise, memorise (with names in a foreign language), organise conceptually - then retrieve and perform in real-time - to have a working literacy of Aikido. No wonder it takes an average ten years to achieve shodan: the memorisation alone is a ten year endeavour.

"We only know the ways we're told, and in the martial arts culture, aren't encouraged to ask if there's a more efficient approach. But, what if we asked? What if we really were designing software? What does the database look like? What kind of decision tree is optimal for performance? How do we optimise the application for both storage and speed?

Where's the 'funnel' through which processes can accelerate?

"Functionally, we need to store, retrieve, and perform, based on these lists:

[attacks]

[movements]

[locations] (omote/ura)

[terminations]

"Right away, we can eliminate [locations], because that information is generally implicit within [movements]: you don't usually perform kotegaeshi omote after having entered with *tenkan* or *taisabaki* body movement. These things carry one naturally ura – and include inertia that you can either use – or have to reverse to move omote. It's not that it's impossible, just that it's not generally efficient – and also likely to offer uke the recovery of *kuzushi*.

"The category with the smallest number of entries, by far, is [movements]. If we can funnel the data through that category, we can dramatically improve efficiency in both storage and retrieval – and therefore learning and performance. And, we can begin to conceptualise Aikido as more of a system rather than a galaxy-scale collection of pairings to memorise. We can establish relationships that not only store the system more efficiently, but that also promote discovery of possibilities we haven't been handed by rote. And, that's the direction, cognitively, I think we want to move ourselves and our students – to move the art."

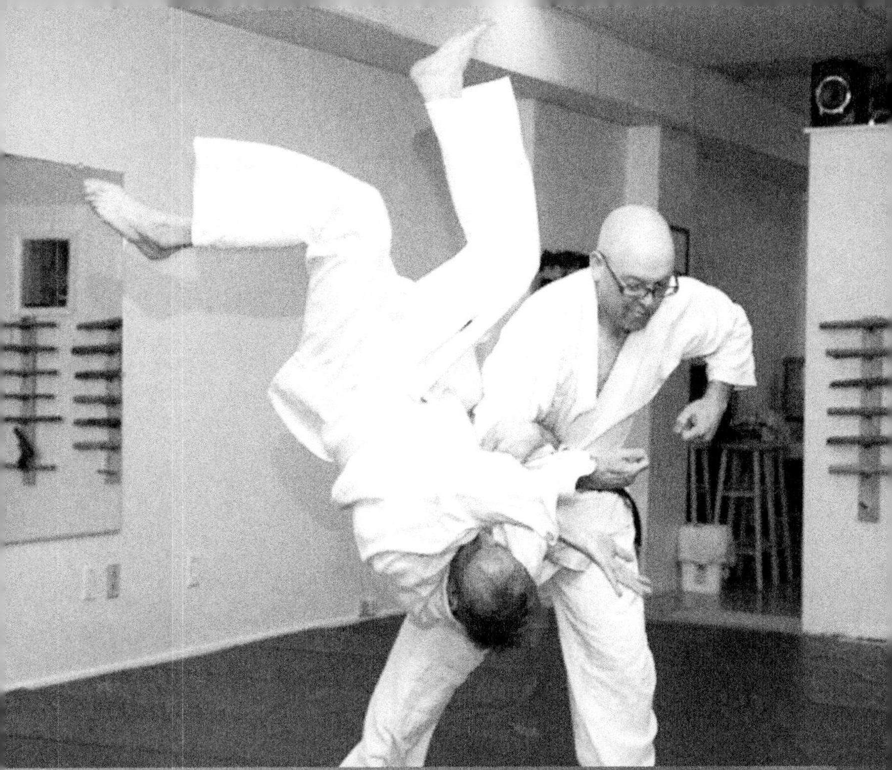

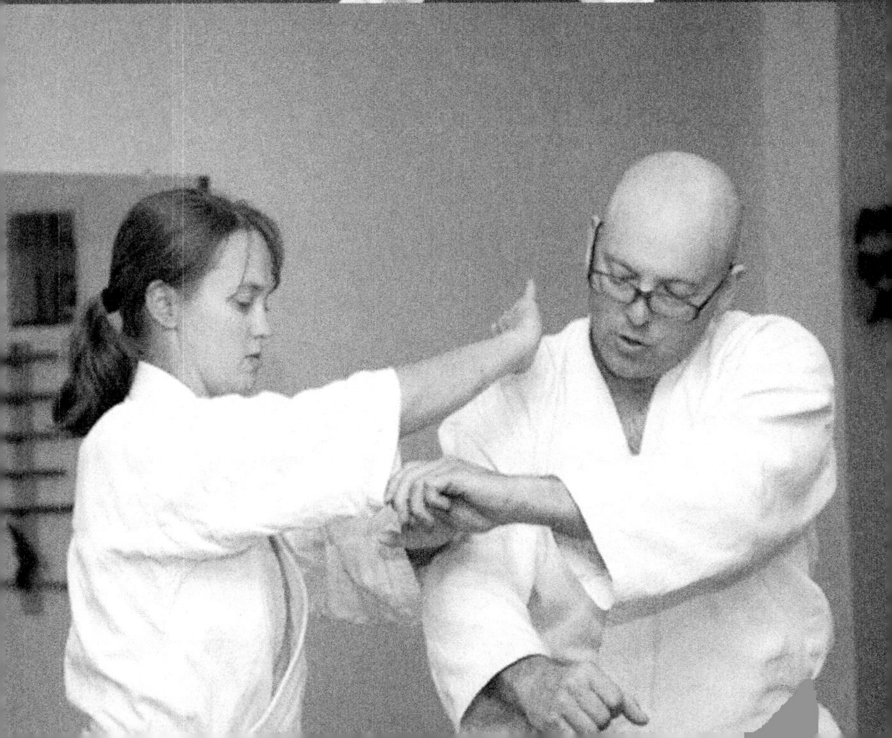

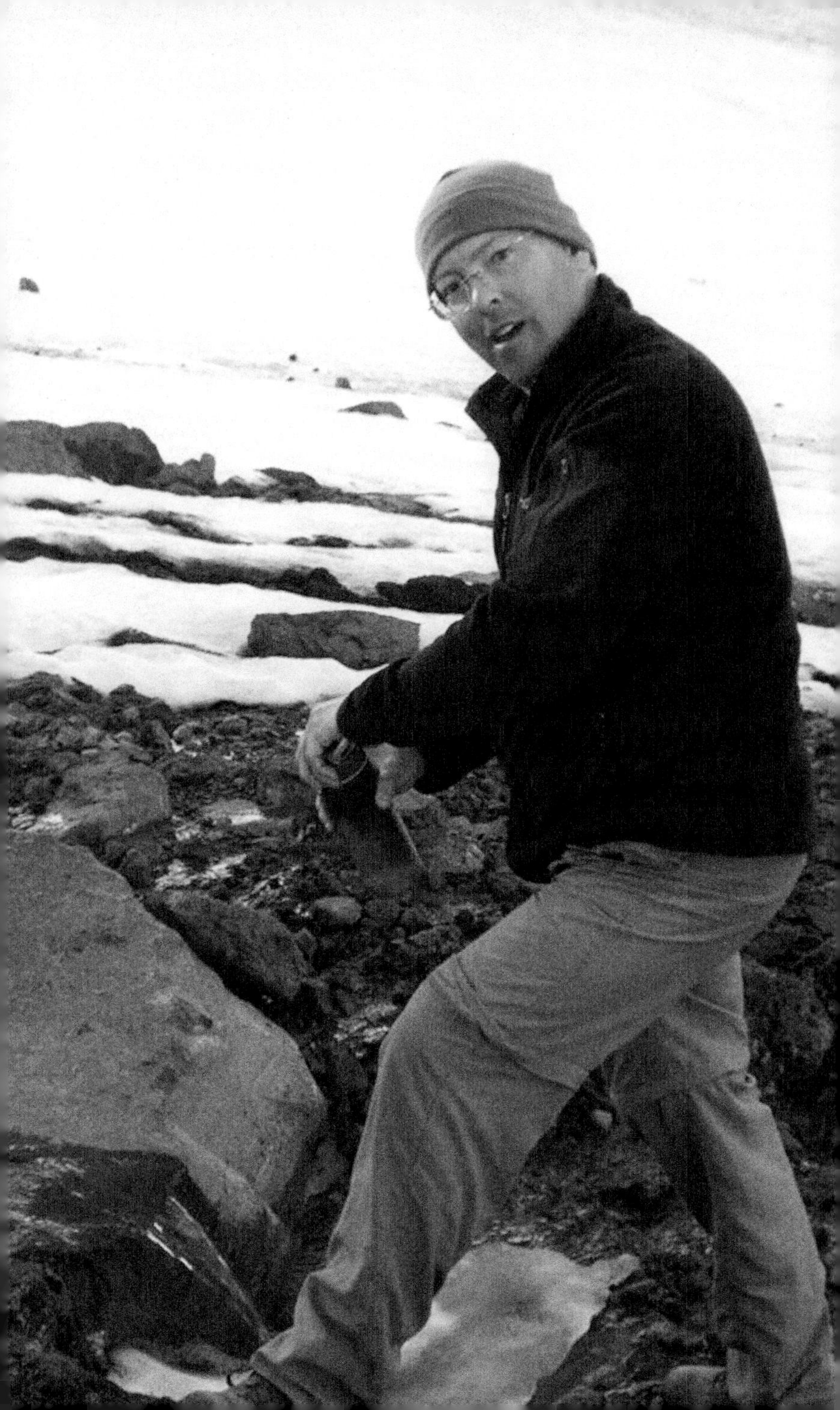

The Domain of Technique Collectors

"I understand that your background includes a career in hands-on work with violent people and training law enforcement. You conjugated academic theory and scientific study with real application. Our environment today is full of prejudices about the Art, and is characterised as much by a non-existent scientific approach to learning tools as by an amount of confusion or outright lies about their application results.

"I read your work and was impressed with your approach and methodology. It shows a holistic vision of Budo training without the traditional constraints of it, while most are learning thousands of techniques as separate entities. I believe that the (many) grey areas in Aikido are just too handy for those teaching it. It's easier to keep drawing letters one by one than to understand how to compose words with them.

"It seems to me that the entire Aikido community is sadly passing down the same didactic mistakes from one generation of students to the next. Then you wonder why someone is accusing contemporary Aikido practice of having become an insipid jam of everything: nobody really knows what they are doing. We are only collecting techniques!

"Glad to find an exception!"

[JB] "Thank you for your kind assessment. I hope it provides some ideas you may find useful to open your own experimentation.

" '*Easier to keep drawing letters one by one than to understand how to compose words with them*', this is an excellent way of putting it. Concerning the current technique collecting habit, Tony Graziano sensei used to say: 'A man with a bag of tricks is not a complete man. If that's all we produce then we are a failure'.

"One of the reasons, I think, Aikido is waning in popularity is that it's becoming a 'dead' art. Most people won't explore the Aikido universe creatively, so they can't use creative methods to teach.

"The material I shared with you is 20 years old now. We have continued with the development of our training methods, adopting and adapting some methods from Filipino martial arts. We also don't do 'polite' randori. We pile uke on top of uke, and carry a percussive fight to them in a randori setting. This is training for the real world. It is dangerous training, even with energy being moderated – which we do.

"Care for training partners can remain paramount while still conducting dynamic and effective training. We've been very happy with the outcome, in reaction times, in the ability to apply *waza* in conflict environments – and also in fun on the mat."

[SC] "Many are starting to ask questions these days. Maybe the lockdown and subsequent inactivity in *Budo* has helped people in rationalising that they have a teaching problem – even though there seem to be very few factual proposals to overcome those problems."

[JB] "I think I would mostly try to answer questions that people may have based on my background from hands-on professional work, to my work as a clinical hypnotist in

With Alan Drysdale

understanding neurological factors, and having spent decades experimenting with different training methods and testing outcomes. Everything I do is science-based, and I recommend to everyone I share with to do quality experimentation – to make a reasonable investment in a method, and to see what the outcomes of that are for their context.

"My personal context has always been both self-protection and self-development. So, we're concerned that things work in the real world, reliably – and, we're concerned with the long-term mental and physical integrity of the practitioner and the dojo community. We train to fight, and we also train with great care for our partners. These things are not mutually exclusive, and in many ways actually synergise.

"This I got from my first two Aikido sensei, one of whom was a SWAT commander and very scary. He once threatened to beat me if I didn't stop going to the local Karate dojo to spar because he said it was going to instil bad habits. At this point in my career, I understand he was right.

" 'Sparring' and 'competing' are not the only ways to train with non-compliant or even combative uke. They are certainly not the best ways, though they can seem 'fun' - at least part of which is ego gratification and (mostly false) confidence-building. The full understanding of this eludes many – and especially those with delicate egos. There are two approaches common to the delicate ego issue:

1. Everything is always gentle and controlled, 'because it's too deadly to practice dynamically'.

2. 'Competition is the only way to ensure it works. What we don't see 'in the cage' is worthless'.

"I see both of these as pandering to ego, and in their own ways manifestations of machinations described in terror management theory. SWAT and Special Forces operators do not kill or injure each other consistently or regularly during training, even with firearms and knives. Yet, they're consistently the winners in real, life-and-death encounters.

"How are you going to practice eyeball-poking technique? Certainly, not in a competitive way...

"The question becomes: 'What ways are there?'

"As far as I can tell, there are few, if any 'Aikido techniques'. For example, every martial art in Asia offers some approximation of kotegaeshi. What makes it 'Aikido'? The answer is: the movement one does before the part we call 'kotegaeshi' - as well as nuances of how it's applied – and the ways practitioners receive the energy of it. The threat to the wrist joint is not special.

"What ways are there to practise what we call 'kotegaeshi' - or anything else we have pasted an Aikido™ name onto?

"There are answers to be found beyond our own experience and history, if we are willing to seek, experiment, and adopt them. Unfortunately, there's a general squeamishness about that – and a magnetic attraction to the familiar – to practice as we always have. In a rut.

"Try abandoning the hakama.

"Try wearing street clothing.

"Try tying your hands together.

"Try tying one hand into the belt.

"Try training in the park, and with shoes on. You will be surprised how much shoes influence your movement, mess with your distancing, force your timing to change.

"Try playing music during practice – something else I took from FMA. Notice that different music enhances different parts of practice – and different types of practice. Notice what happens to timing, spontaneously, if you simply play heavily syncopated music in the background while training. Music has a powerful influence on our cognition, processing, and emotional/performance state.

"Try giving NAGE the tanto: then, attack katate dori - grabbing nage's wrist the way someone might to try to arrest the knife-hand on the street. From there practise all the standard katate dori curriculum, using the knife in the ways that present themselves. This one experiment, done with curiosity and intention, can shine a light into the deep and dark corners of the real Budo of which most of Aikido is now a faint shadow.

"We have several training methods, some adapted from FMA practices, that are standard parts of our practice – and all of which were formed through curiosity and experimentation, asking: 'What would that sound like in the language of Aikido?'

"A friend with whom I used to train Kali used to say something like: 'The job of sensei is to conceal the repetition of training – to protect from tedium, to keep the view and the approach fresh and exciting'. If this is all we achieve, then the variations are worthy, though what we really want is to find 'best practices' and to continually escape our comfort (tedium) zone. Because that last bit is what Budo is really about."

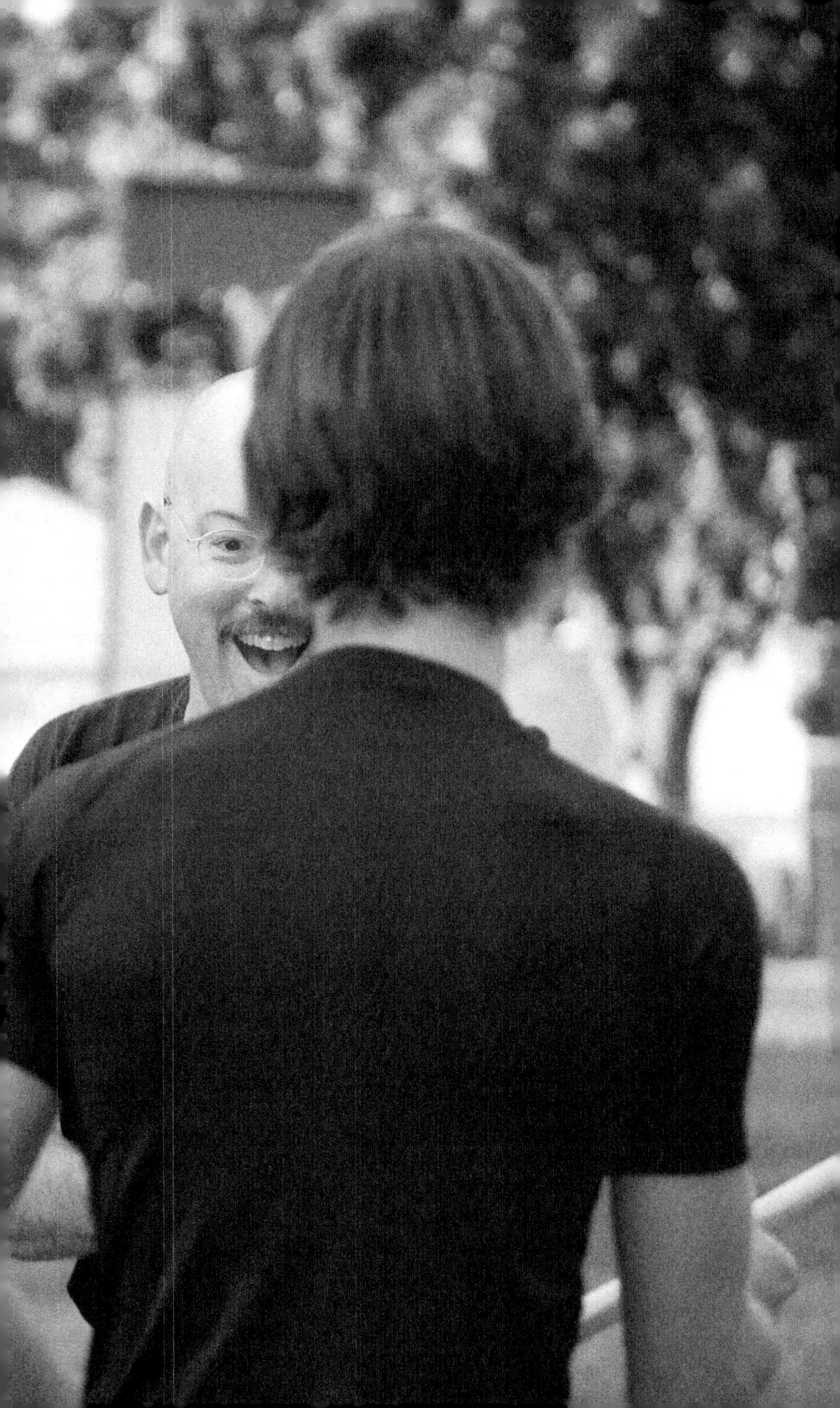

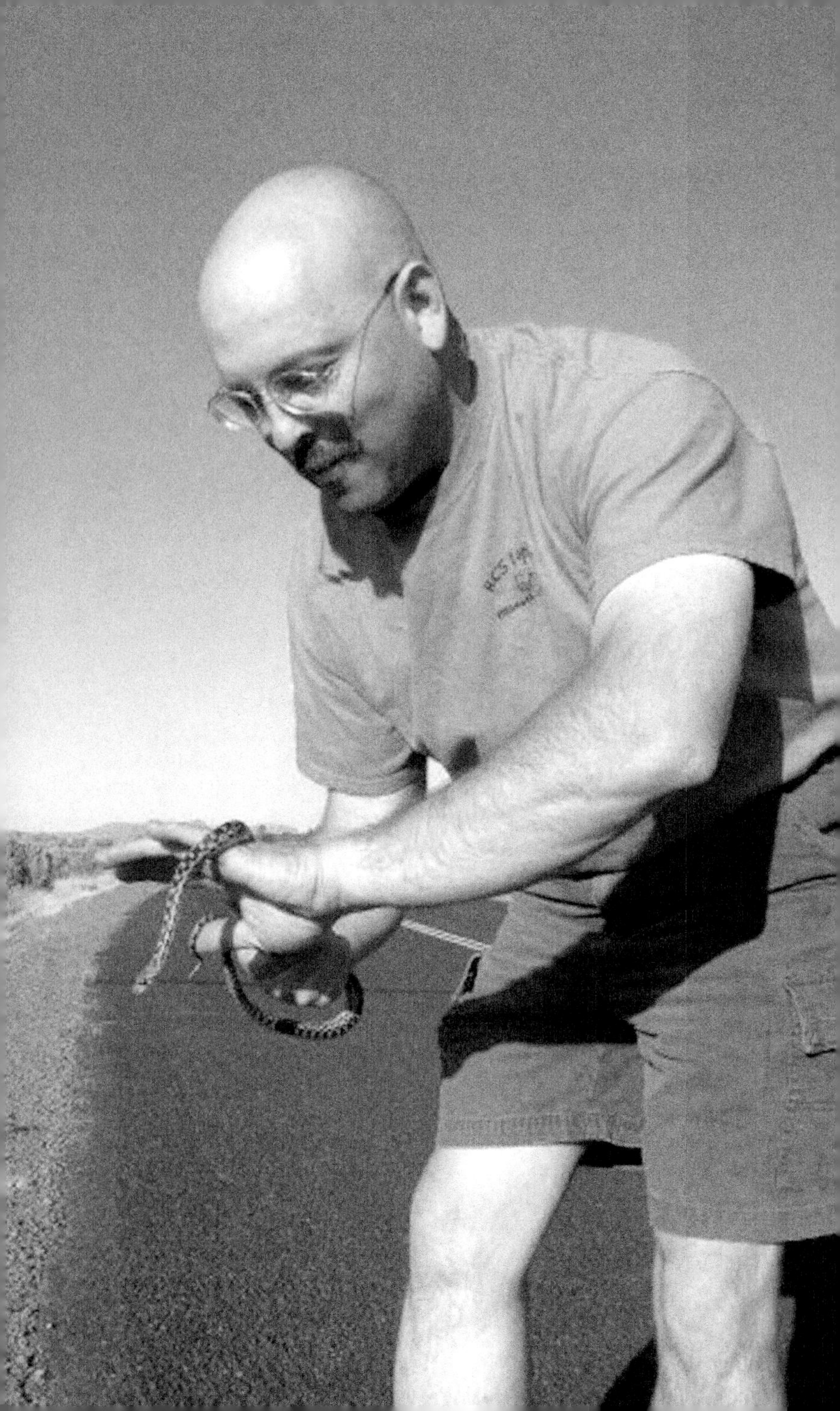

A Verifiable Approach

"A verifiable approach, maybe not necessarily an exhaustive one, is somewhere to start from. The swamp of pseudo-Ueshiba pacifism of the last two decades has left, in my opinion, a great void. At best, everyone is trying to repeat stuff that they or their teacher have seen from a Japanese shihan in the '70s or '80s. There is no clear sense of path and progression. If we look at all the different Aikido associations, they have one approach only: 'Simply do this and the certificates will keep coming'."

[JB] "Everyone has their own criteria for practising 'martial arts'. Many have their own idea of what they even are. I think that being clear about outcomes, and understanding that in the frame of 'well formed outcome' is a necessary beginning.

"Past that, I think that what one can probably produce – and also probably transmit to others – can be called 'a system'. If only one person – or just a few extraordinary persons – can do something, it isn't really 'a system'. This concept came from Tom Walker sensei: 'You are only as good as what you can pass along'.

"One of the concepts I talk about often – and explicitly, when I teach – is the 'level of contrivance'. ALL 'training' is an interaction that is to some extent contrived or constrained. Even in randori, we don't kick-out knees, or groynes – or gouge eyes. And, in most dojo, it's considered wrong to throw uke ONTO or INTO each other. Most Aikido practice is done at a high level of contrivance: *kata* with a partner.

"One of the things that are missing in traditional Aikido practice is a method for bridging from high contrivance to relatively low contrivance. We look at the learning curve and the stress when people first begin randori…"

[SC] "It is meaningless for Aikido teachers to continuously point out that Ueshiba sensei supposedly did this and that, when we cannot. How can you base a teaching system on outcomes you cannot reproduce?"

[JB] "Precisely."

[SC] "It also leaves the door open to all sorts of baloney to justify how to get to what he was doing and we are not."

[JB] "I cross-trained with people from Filipino systems that have a strong intermediate-contrivance practice that bridges the gap. I stole the methods, adapted them to Aikido. This is much of the material I've been working on in the 20 years since the book material I shared with you.

"On your notes about Ueshiba… People often ask me about 'the spiritual side'… And, I ask 'of breaking someone's arm?'

"I explain how easily *sankyo osae* breaks the arm. I've done it multiple times. I explain how it sounds; how it feels when you snap another human's bones in your hands. Not very 'spiritual'. Not what they were seeking.

"Then, I talk about the emotional factors afterwards. And, that's what they're concerned about – wanting to be 'effective' but never suffer spiritually/emotionally from

Morihei Ueshiba

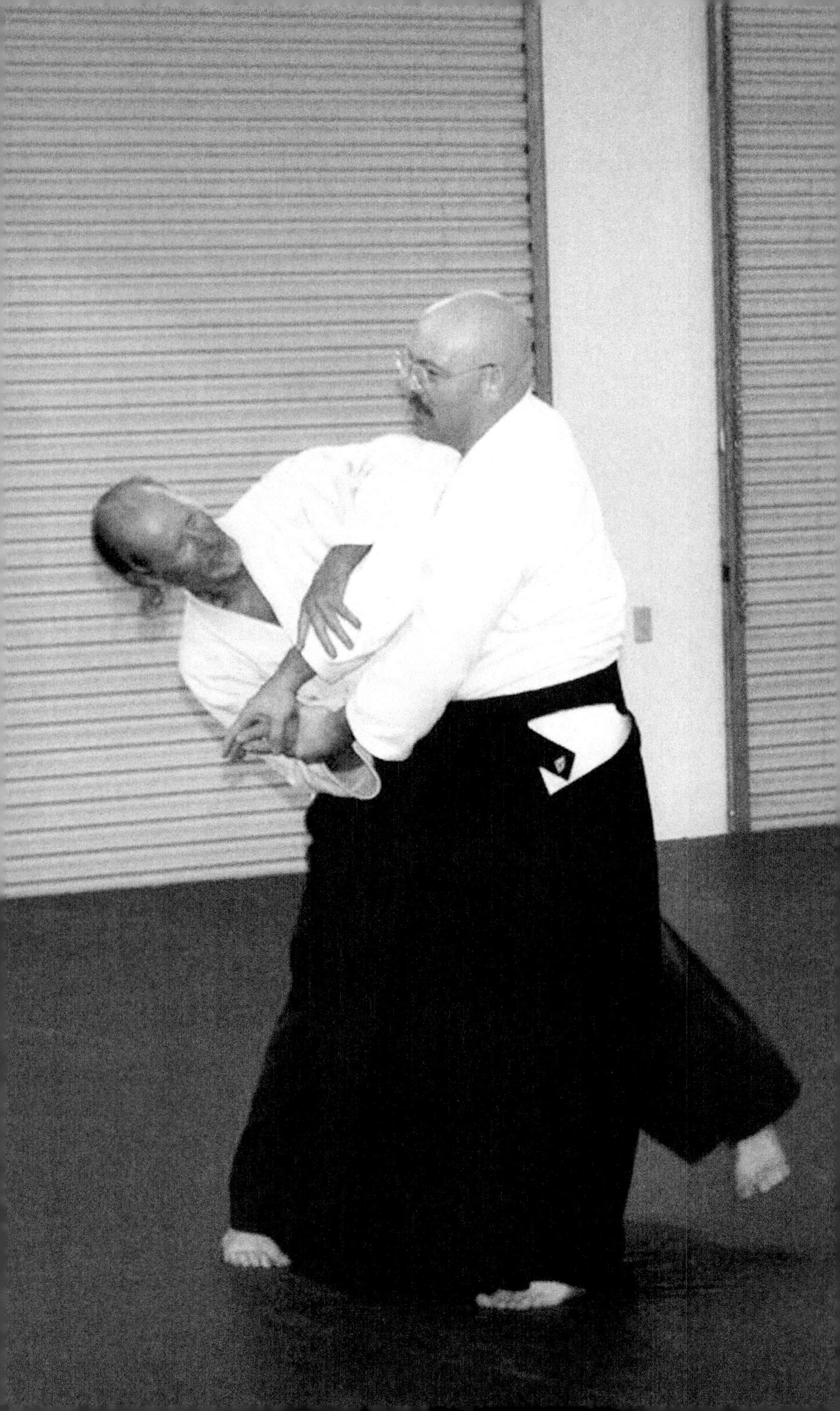

having harmed someone else. The discussion deepens...

"My personal conclusion, and structurally, is that 'mercy' or 'benevolence' has a prerequisite of credible destructive capacity. Without that prerequisite, it's a facade. And, a facade one presents to oneself is a delusion. To me, the purest 'real' Aikido is doing one's best not to cause undue harm – and when the aggression of an attack literally (not figuratively or philosophically) rebounds to the attacker to cause them the injury."

[SC] "You can't offer mercy if you don't know how to not to. To be harmonious, you must know disharmony and decide not to go there."

[JB] "Yes. To me, Aikido contains a large number of 'booby traps' – where an opening seems available to a would-be aggressor – but if they pursue it with commitment and intent, they will break their own body. The most direct example of this I think is sankyo osae.

"The first time I broke someone's arm, I saw they were going to pursue the punch, and I tried my best to release the sankyo. I was moving to *chikaku* and I was safe from the punch because of my positioning. I suspected they would be injured and did my best to release them. They were very fast – and very committed – faster than I could release...

"The arm broke like a pencil in my hand, with a stunningly small amount of force. I was in a professional environment and fighting hands-on every day. I was not adrenalised at all. Very calm. So, I wasn't over-muscling, etc."

[SC] "The aggressor broke himself."

[JB] "Exactly that. I felt very bad and, as a consequence, I became quite skilled with *yonkyo*. That was my adaptation. Today, I see the event as a very pure 'aiki' concept playing-out in physical reality."

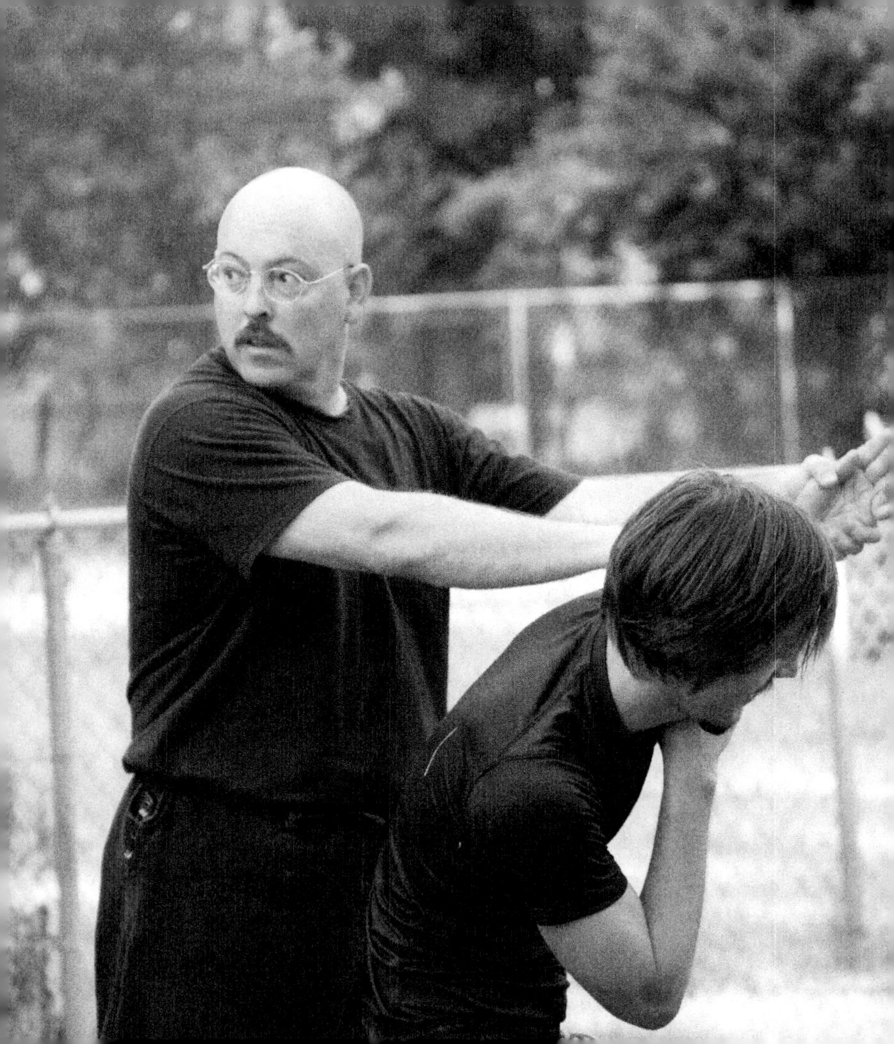

Bones Can Snap

"Do you realise that this bone snapping talk cannot be digested by mainstream Aikido? People have built a fantasy world where Budo is possible without harming and being harmed by simply de-constructing every martial aspect of training. This is why today Aikido is so often an empty dance mimicking medieval Japanese martial applications."

"Yes, and it's difficult to have the conversation around 'real application' – in part because many people doing hands-on violence professionally – or who have – are wrestling with demons around it. They tend to have a frightful (from fearful) outlook and presentation. To me, it's a departure in the opposite direction. To me, this is where 'self-development' begins to show itself – not in terms of mere physical strength, flexibility, skill – but on the psychological plane – in terms of reconciling all that our humanity really entails – which includes binocular vision, canine teeth, tribalism, territoriality, etc. Denial of these things is not 'development' but delusion. Suppression of them is not 'developmental' – and not part of RECONCILING them.

"This is where credible and martial factors are an integral part of 'development' – for which there are no shortcuts past the dark places. Fixation on them – or being enthralled by them – is a pathology. Likewise, denial or repression. They must be dealt with appropriately.

"That's an entire collection of challenges – of different kinds, whether one goes out and does violence professionally – or one wants to never experience that outside a controlled dojo. On one path lies dangers of PTSD, moral injury, physical injury – or just becoming a violent person. On the other hand, various delusional nonsense."

[SC] "And the psychological abuse of both self and students. Aikido is a perfect hiding place for sneaky abusers who do not like to risk being challenged. Many teachers or seniors in it are like this: semi abusers on a physical and psychological level."

[JB] "My sensei was Tom Walker. He came up in a very harsh dojo. He could be a bear to take ukemi for but was never abusive. He just DID Aikido.

"He had a rift from one of the big organisations and sent me to a seminar by the senior student of one of the other Shihan, to feel-out their general way of doing things. The guy was a perfect example of what you describe – cruel to a teen-aged student to the point we walked out of the seminar.

[SC] "And that is the true face of a good few seniors in Aikido who, behind their peaceful words, hide all their unsolved issues – after decades of training in a supposed conflict resolution art."

[JB] "You see a great deal of that garbage in people who profess 'real Aikido' – or 'effective', etc. It's one of the things we have to contend with – also because we integrate a load of percussive techniques. There can be a perception that it's 'harsh'. We don't do it abusively, but rather carefully – and emphasise that ukemi is inherently the practice to manage being struck.

"This gets to some of the videos of O-sensei, where people say uke were jumping for him. They were in many cases evading the strike he had shown them was there – could be there – and which might be if they stuck their nose over there.

"Aikido 'works' in many ways based on strikes – or uke's response to a strike – that's NEVER shown – and that many 'sensei' don't even know is there. You have to explore that part of the art to even know what's there (or not). And, you can not do in the real world what you never practise. So, it's necessary to practise – which doesn't mean brutalising your partner, either.

"I have a principle that I teach (and enforce) – that one may not apply a technique with more speed and energy beyond one's own demonstrated ability to absorb it, comfortably. Of course, we don't want to apply a technique beyond what our uke can absorb safely – but I've discovered the rule I outlined seems to prevent people doing that because it keeps them attentive to the ukemi side of the interaction."

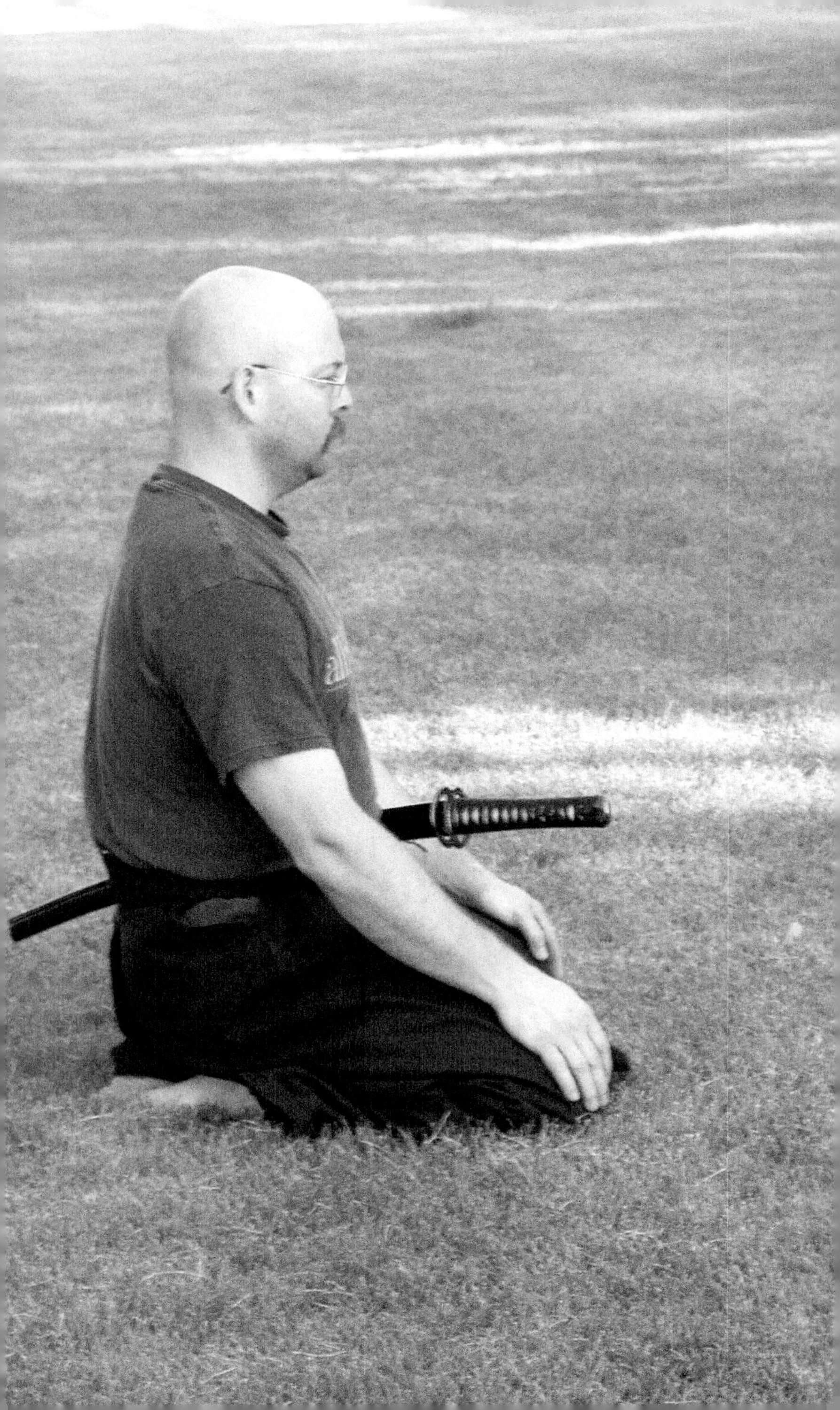

Not Enough Time

"Maybe there is not enough time spent training for both students and teachers to develop anything? Modern lifestyle doesn't exactly help personal development after all. And if the training methods are old, confused and cumbersome, that development may never come."

"I think there's plenty of time available. I think three classes a week are plenty for progression. I think time is not efficiently used. Too much formality, for one thing – sucks up time.
"Another issue: number of iterations of stimulus-response. High levels of contrivance reduce this count. Possible solutions?
"Balance of practice at different levels of contrivance. We typically see 90+% of a training month spent in the highest levels of contrivance. Low iteration count, and a semi-static type of energy/interaction. The simple shift into intermediate levels of contrivance can 5x or even 10x stimulus-response iterations, the ability to work with more dynamic energy, and more importantly the ability to bring techniques from 'live' interactions.

[SC] "Again, you are pointing out that the standard or

'traditional' tools would not be adequate. Do you think that mainstream Aikido will ever conceive abandoning icons like Aikido etiquette and the traditional technique names, just to name two? Or getting rid of the attire or all the typical rites that punctuate an Aikido class? Most would probably tell you that that's what Budo is really about. Personally, I really doubt it will ever happen."

[JB] "Aikido is all about flexibility, right?"

[SC] "It is not! [Laughs]. The more people get up the ladder, the less they become available for change, even though they teach it verbally on a daily basis."

[JB] "I think that in *The Magic of Aikido* I quoted O-sensei about building on the foundations and adapting new forms. In the book I also covered the naming convention problems. All of that is just science and proven outcomes.

"Tom Walker sensei used to talk about the '2% rule' – that only 2% of most people in a given profession are excited enough about it to constantly seek adaptation and innovation and improvement. Everyone else just wants to punch the clock, go through the motions, and collect their 'pay' – even if it's social. He said this applied to Aikido as well.

"I think this is not a reason to remain with one's feet stuck in the concretion of 'tradition' – which really means 'dogma and sloth', from my POV.

"It's interesting to see the degree of resistance to simply arranging the words differently (again, material in my book) – to practising the exact same movements in a different order or organisation. It's interesting, the degree of resistance to doing something more dynamic and interactive not instead of, but in addition to, the higher level of contrivance formalised movements.

"I've tried to promote these ideas to people I know – into

the old dojo that persisted after my sensei passed. I've taught some of this stuff there. It was received with interest, curiosity, etc – but was not adopted or integrated.

"Comfortable" must be understood as equivalent to 'boring' - and as the antithesis of 'training'. If we can possibly recall the times when we were, mathematically, making the most rapid progress in our learning, those were the least-comfortable times of our martial arts career. We were frustrated, possibly frightened. We had physical and mental discomfort.

"Then, at some point, we begin to settle-in to a comfortable pattern – to sleep-walk through the routine. And, that maintains some level of physical flexibility and fitness, but it calcifies the mind."

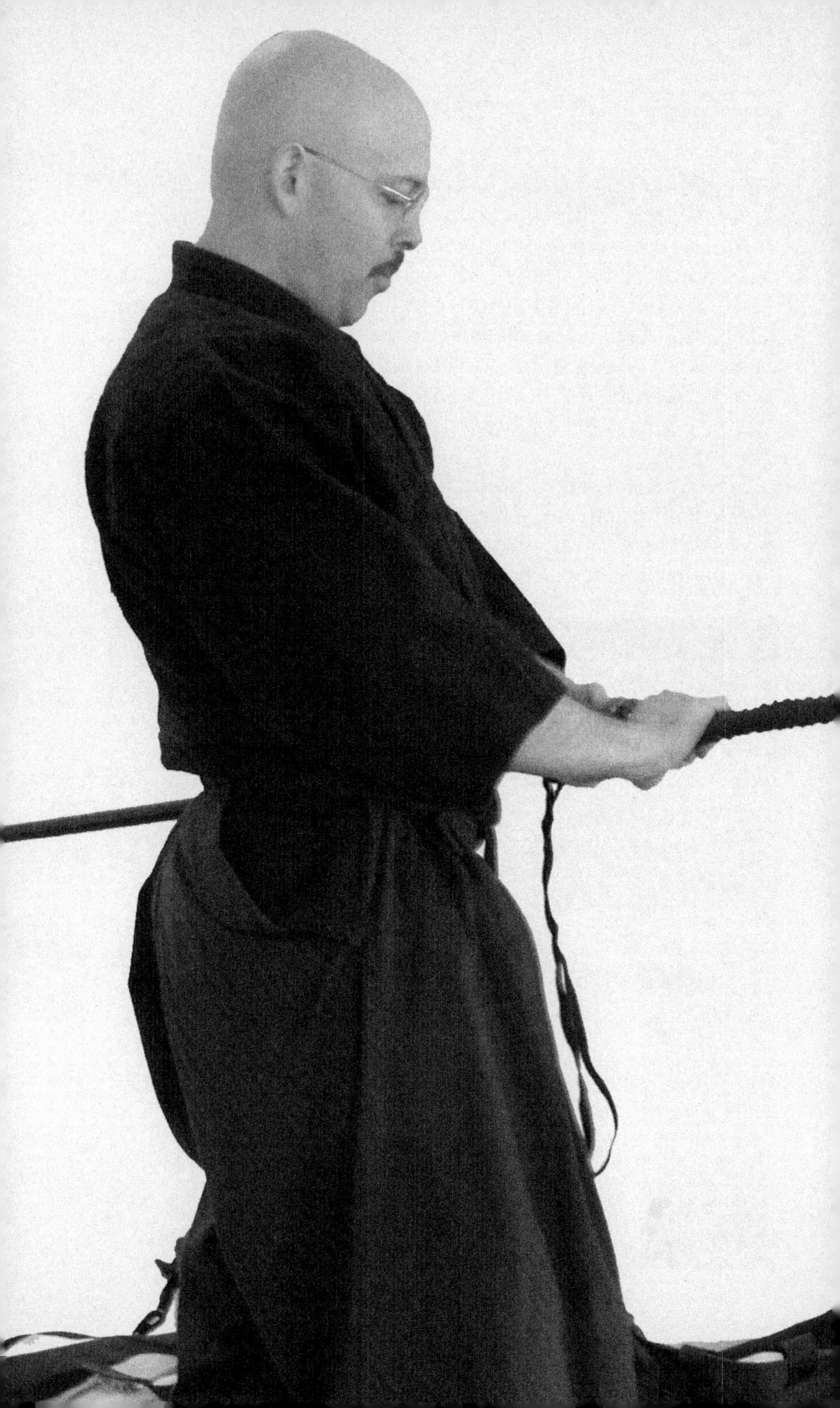

The Naming Convention Issue in Aikido

"In your book you are suggesting that the naming convention in Aikido is co-responsible for the slow or inadequate progression of the learner. Could you explain why?"

"Language is the software of the human mind. The ways in which we language a thing both create and disclose the inner processing of that thing. Much of our communication gets carried in the empty spaces of our language.

"If I say: 'katate dori – kotegaeshi' - what must you do to comprehend it?

"You don't know if I mean *gyaku* hand or *ai* hand.

"You don't know if I mean to do taisabaki, tenkan, or what we call 'male triangle' (omote-type footwork). Or did I mean *irimi* footwork?

"Look at the massive amount of processing you have to do – and the time that takes - just to organise ideas of what I MIGHT mean. Imagine being asked to teach a (somewhat) complete list of what can be called 'katate dori – kotegaeshi' - in a single class…

"If you have a respectable physical vocabulary of Aikido, you can't fit that into a single class period. That's pretty obviously inefficient. I think what we inherited as

The Innovator

curriculum, and naming conventions are the attempt to catalogue and describe the sweeping singular genius that was O-sensei. And, I think these performance science and education concepts weren't available or weren't considered.

"Let's look at the software – the subroutines we see, either explicitly or implicitly, in the standard naming convention.
1. Recognize there's some threat. We explicitly dictate this in the naming convention for e.g. 'katate d o r i – kotegaeshi'.
2. Make some movement to escape. (implicit)
3. Move to chikaku. (implicit)
4. Make some attachment to uke. (implicit)
5. Manipulate uke in some manner, beginning with breaking their balance, and ending with some osae or nage waza. (the 'kotegaeshi' part of the name)

"Let's call it those five steps for the traditional naming convention.

"Then, let's look at code optimisation – what's really necessary, and how can we make it more efficient just by talking about it (encoding it) differently.

"Beginning the naming convention with the specific attack implies we must identify the specific attack as step 1. And, because the other half of the naming convention is step 5 – it is neurologically necessary to locate and load all of the code necessary for the intervening steps PRIOR to beginning our execution. (That's how neurology works.)

"This is massively inefficient.

"We don't need to identify the specific threat. I don't need to know the train is the 3:10 to Yuma; I just need to get off the tracks before it hits me.

"The literal most-important bit of the entire system is item 2: Escape the impact zone – what military operators call 'getting off the X'.

"And, that's the part of the naming convention that

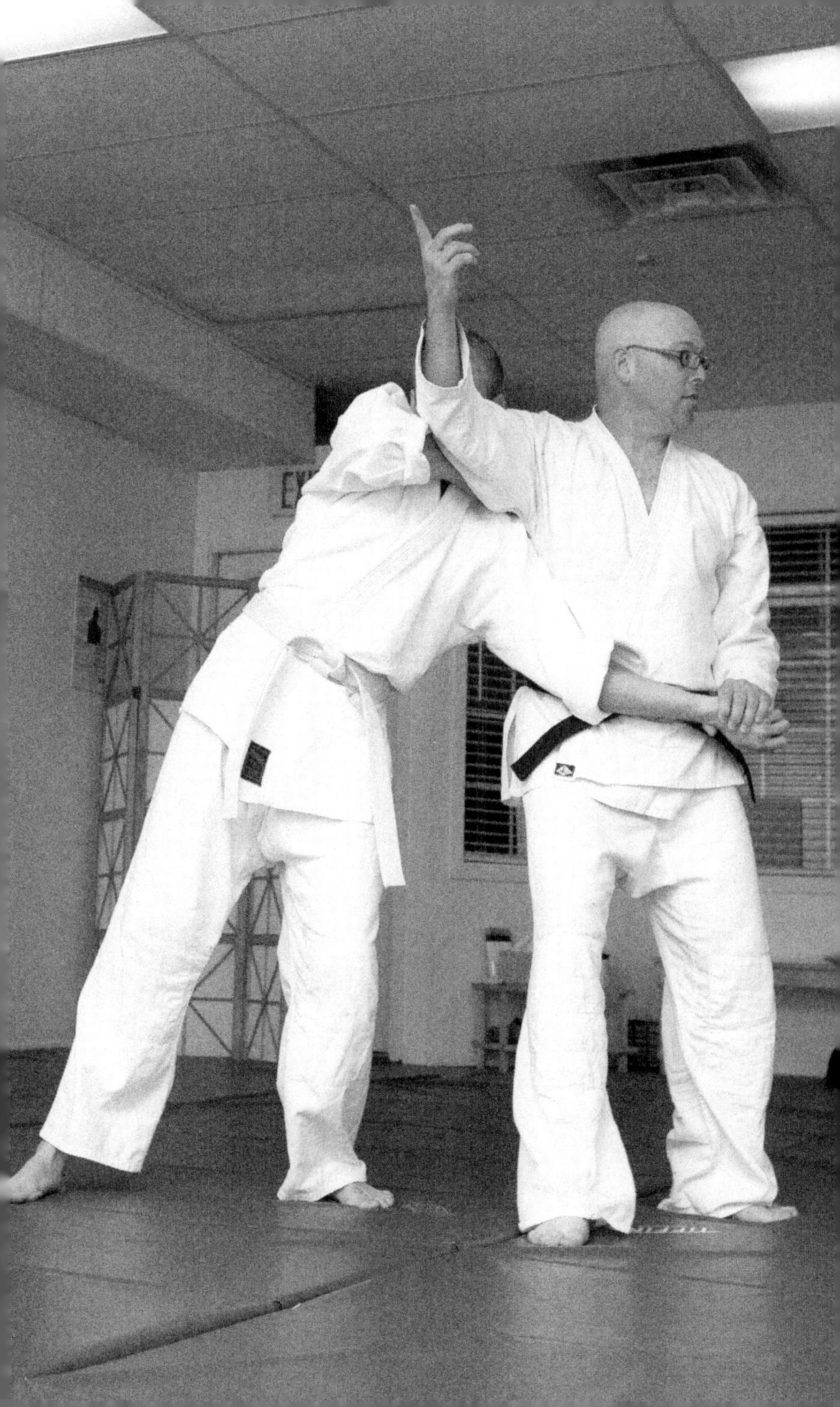

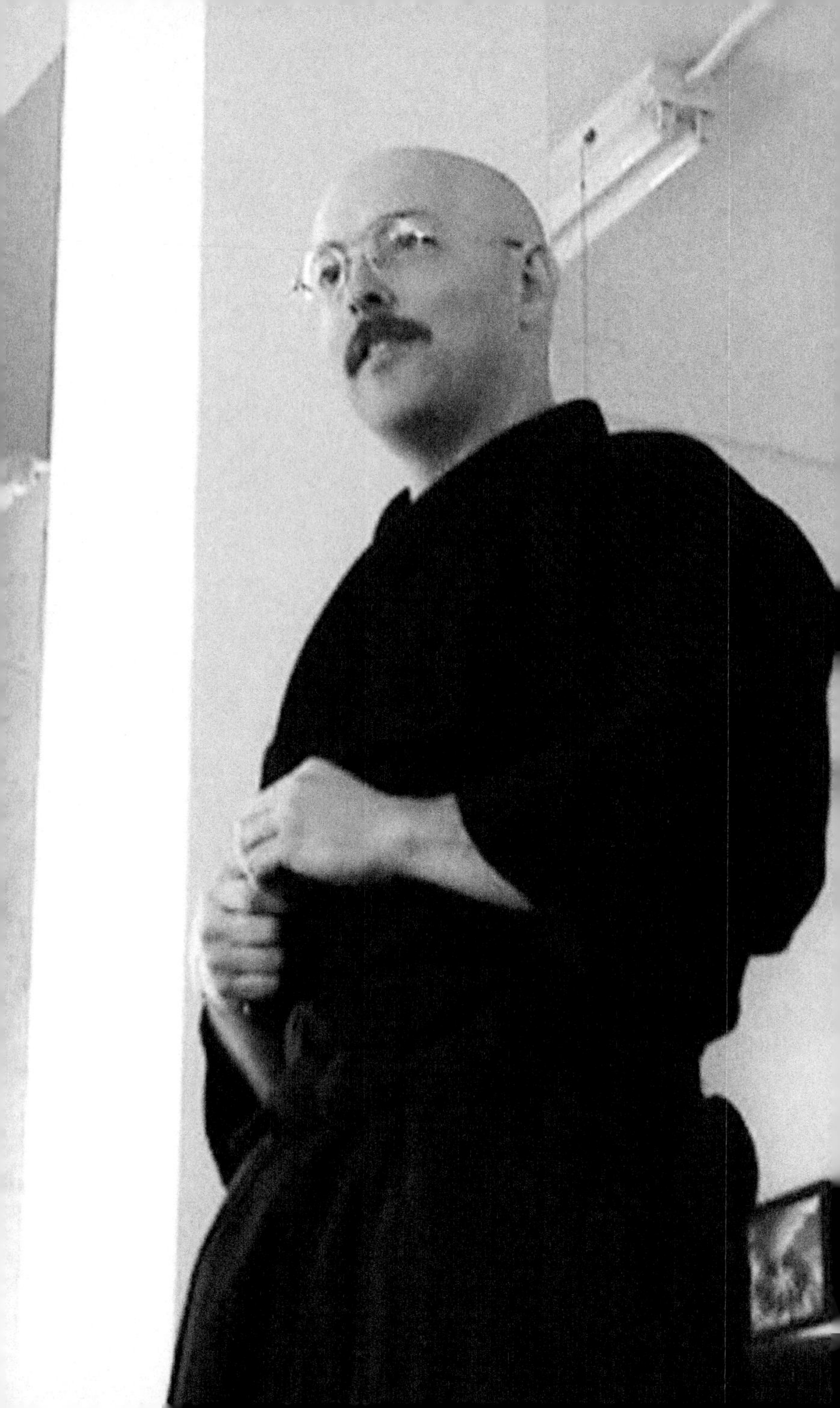

The Innovator

mostly does not exist – and that when it's given, it's provided AFTER the attack-termination structure, e.g. 'katate dori – kotegaeshi' - and almost as an afterthought, 'ura form'. This still isn't really explicit, because 'ura' and 'omote' are not body movements or foot works, but locations relative to uke.

"The most important part of the whole system – in fact, the part that's unique to Aikido (kote gaeshi isn't) – is the part we don't, as a practice, explicitly encode.

"If you fail at this mostly-unnamed part you will not reach chikaku; you can not really do Aikido – even if you twist someone's wrist. Though, you probably will also not twist their wrist because they will be punching you while you're focused on the wrist instead of where you are in space relative to their lines of power.

"Why will you focus on twisting their wrist while they are punching you?

"Because, we understand that what is encoded in language is important, and focus attention on it. We're focusing on 'kote gaeshi' - and not on movement or on chikaku – the things we didn't even speak to.

"This is long-winded to write down. And, to read.

"We're breaking down the encoding and retrieval of software in the way the brain is processing it – and in the ways the brain is interpreting hierarchy of importance according to the implications contained in the language – by what is said, and what is not (seemingly worth being) mentioned.

"And, some people will say their instructor emphasises movement and position – and above termination.

"Yes. Mine, too – probably more than anyone else.

"Yet, the structure leads us to build a giant library of permutations of very long neural programs – that take a (relatively) long time to retrieve and load before they can begin executing. And, those neural programs include a large amount of overhead of fine motor function like picking up the hand and placement of the fingers – that are utterly

The Innovator

unnecessary to just getting out of the way of that oncoming train (gross motor function).

"The language outlined strongly presses us toward unnecessarily large, slow, unwieldy neural programs, while literally ignoring the most important – and the only Aikido-unique part.

"Scientifically, we want to focus on our evasive manoeuvre. This is the gunfighter's draw. We need it to be as fast as possible – exiting the target zone and moving toward chikaku as the goal of program 1.

"We also want to segregate coding for the termination from the movement component. Combining the two – which the old naming convention implicitly does - leads to code-bloat, and therefore reaction-time bloat."

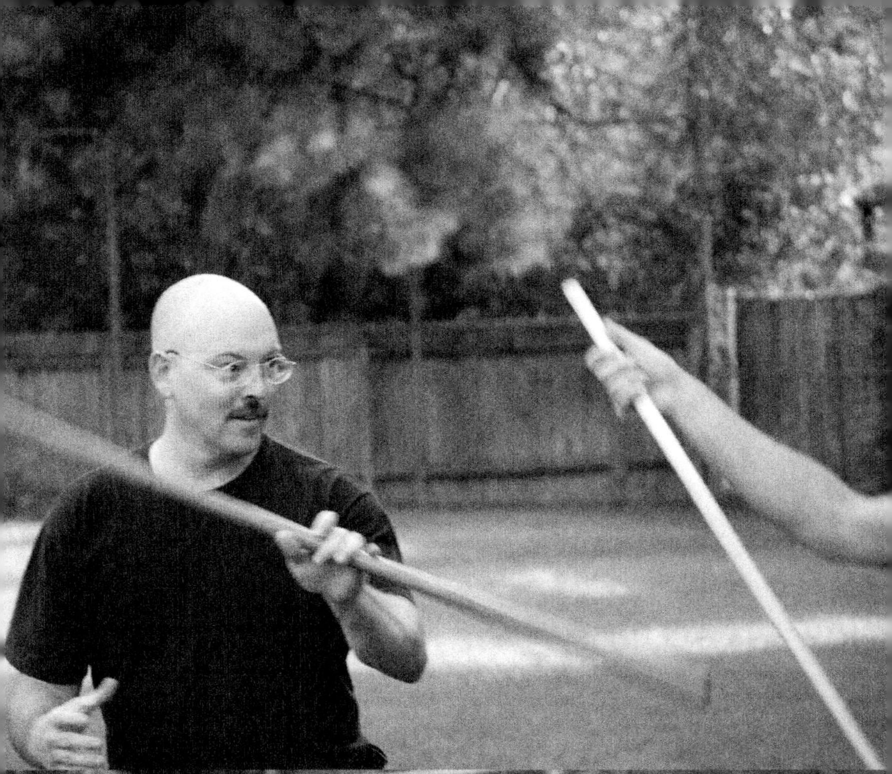
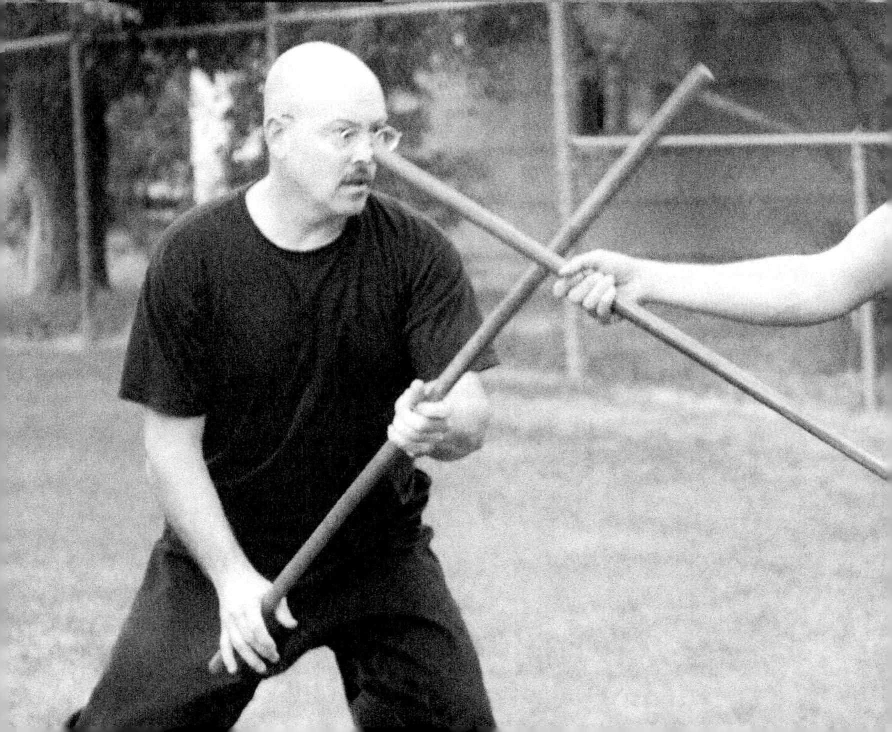

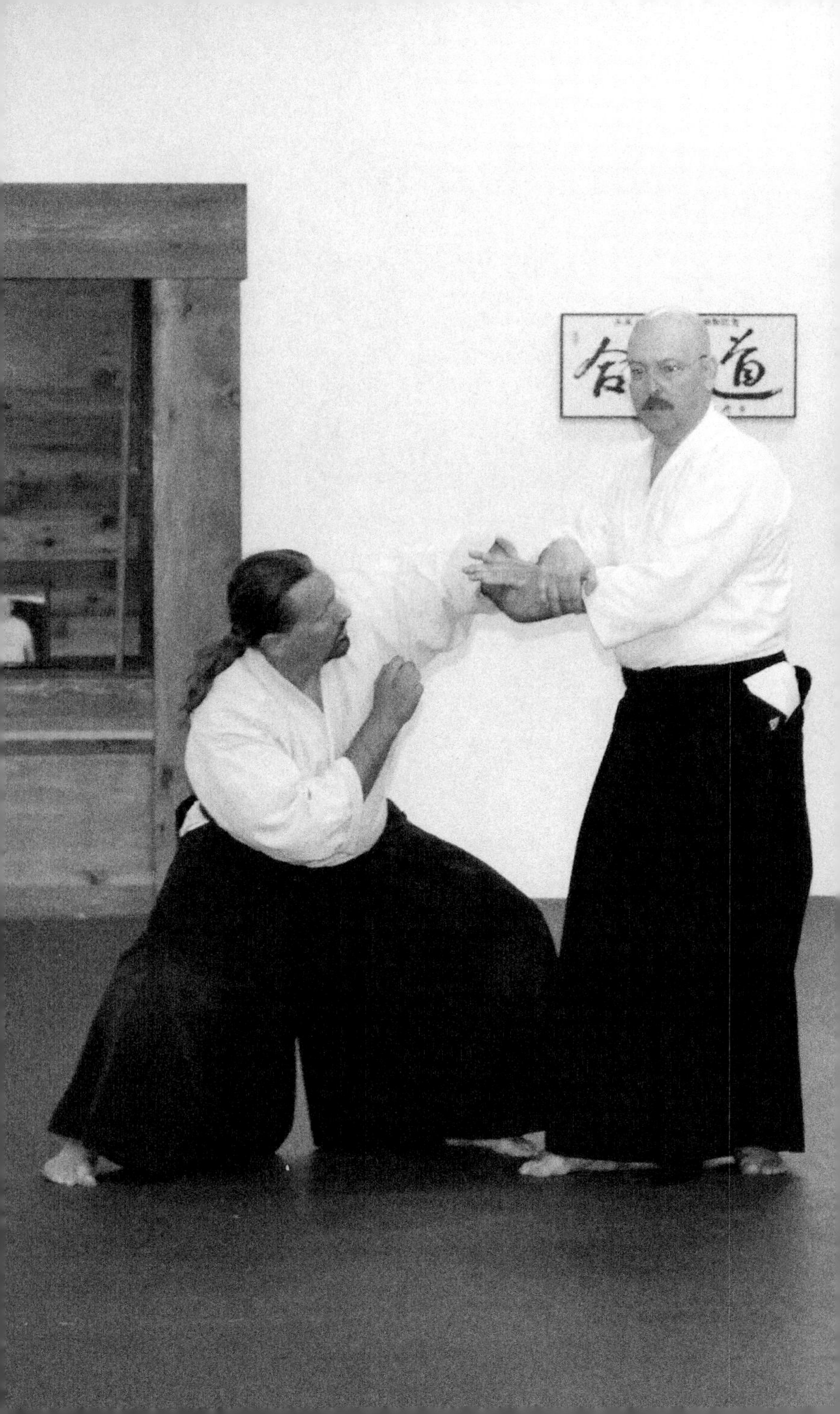

Generalisation vs Specification

"In the natural world, generalisation has the specific function of helping to learn faster. In martial arts, however, the methodology is based on specialisation, which leads to a slowing down of the learning process. Based on your research, could you expand on those two areas and explain how they relate to improving our Aikido?"

"John Boyd stated that all conflict is a time-competitive OODA cycle (observe-orient-decide-act) – and that the party who consistently completes the cycle faster will usually win.

"We know that both in learning and in performing, generalisation is faster than specification. And, we know from Hick's law of motor learning that every branch in our decision tree (each requirement for specification/differentiation forces a branch) we will roughly double our reaction time.

"So, to the extent practical, it is advantageous to employ generalisation rather than specification.

"It's this principle, and this science I'm talking about in evaluating the old naming convention – and designing a new one. If we think it necessary to identify the specific attack prior to loading and firing the reaction program customised to that attack, we'll suffer reaction time inflation due to code bloat.

"The magic of Aikido is that the movement patterns unique to the art allow us to generalise initial reaction programs and to load termination programs afterward.

"I believe that's the cognitive magic that allowed O-sensei to seem untouchable. I think it's what many higher-level Aikidoka come to do intuitively at some point. The naming and teaching conventions we operate under just don't promote that efficiency.

"I realised this while watching a Russian aikidoka named Igor Taratin doing a really great randori. He stopped throwing and did only body movement – in close quarters and uke working at full throttle. We've seen that done by some really advanced aikidoka before. The difference was he used only one body movement – taisabaki.

"During that time, in about 1994, I was writing some data compression algorithms. So, though Taratin sensei didn't explicitly teach this generalisation of one body movement to any possible attack, I immediately realised the data compression and code optimisation I was witnessing.

"The cognitive shortcut: he wasn't identifying the attack before moving; he wasn't planning a termination. He was just doing explosive evasion. And, a single body movement worked no matter what the uke brought him. It took me some time to design and implement the compression, but it's become a core principle for us. Bruce Lee taught the principle of 'economy of motion'. This is that principle, applied to 'mental motion'.

"The process led us to notice that terminations can also be compressed, and that practising them in those patterns enhances learning of related techniques. For example, ai katate dori *ikkyo* omote waza is a nearly identical movement to a form of *kokyunage*: just move everything from the ai-side arm to gyakyu-side arm. Likewise, ai katate dori *ude kime* nage omote waza is the same as gyaku katate dori *sumi otoshi*.

"And, there are many other terminations that can be learned faster through generalising – and by practising them in these patterns we call 'mirrored pairs'.

"We organise the termination part of our curriculum not according to the initial attack, but according to the positional relationship with uke after the entrance. This organisation results in massive data compression of the volume of 'Aikido techniques'.

"Past all of the mentioned advantages, there's another: pre-loading the response program. This is a departure from the magical concept of *mushin*: we know that any well-executed Aikido body movement is likely to escape or reduce the effects of any attack uke launches. So, we get to decide which movement we want to use. The final issue is just timing – when to fire the program. The strategy of preloading a neural program is proven to significantly reduce reaction time, which is especially important when operating at close (conversational) *maai*.

"Finally, considering randori, preloading entrance movement allows us to plan at a more strategic level. We can choose our movement tactically, according to the layout of the room, rather than having it dictated by the random attack of the nearest uke – the latter being another thing we set up by using the traditional naming convention.

"All of this is modern war-fighting doctrine (John Boyd), meets neuroscience (Hicks, et al), meets data compression theory and code optimization, meets a (sometimes) 2-for-1 advantage in techniques-per-hour of training."

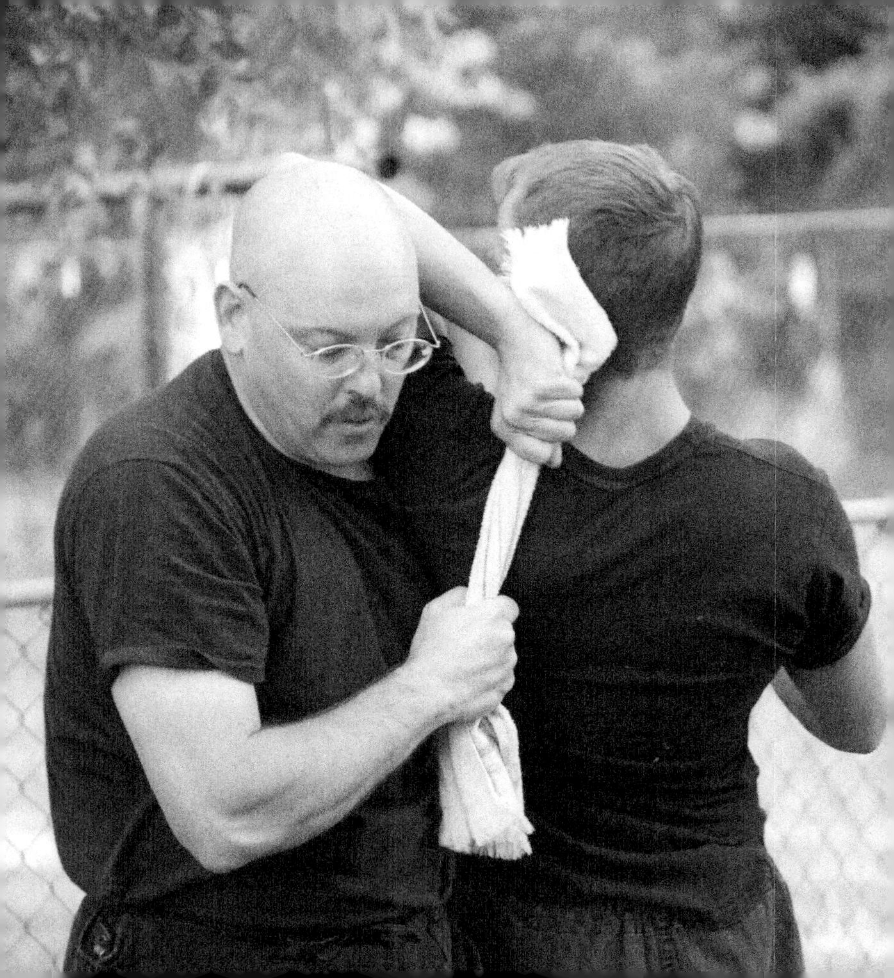

The Way of Uke

"What is your view of the role of uke in Aikido?"

"Literal translation of 'ukemi' is approximately 'receiving body'. It is, in my opinion, the entire basis for Aikido. We can only 'blend' or 'harmonise' with that which we can receive. So, all Aikido begins with ukemi – the mind, body, and spirit of safely 'receiving' some possibly-dangerous energy.

"I say 'A person with sufficiently powerful ukemi needs no waza'. Such a person would be invincible by avoiding, escaping, evading, deflecting, or even absorbing - anything thrown at them. This is the beginning of our explanation of Aikido and ukemi.

"The 'role' of uke is more complex than the role of nage. Uke must play their role with what Chiba shihan called 'sincerity' - in the service of nage's training and progress. In some ways, rather than 'receiving', uke are 'giving' themselves – their energy, their body – in service of the technique.

"Uke must be neither excessively nor insufficiently powerful, fast, or resistant. The best learning curves involve the right amounts of frustration – and possibly even fear. Uke must 'give' to service that for their partner to their best ability, while also protecting themselves from harm. Once one becomes sufficiently advanced, the best way to study a technique is by taking ukemi for it.

"At Executive Security International, I started out as one of the slowest drivers on the track. We all think we can drive fast, but the first hairpin curve as a passenger of instructor Steve Bigelow scared the hell out of me. And, although I came along, it was my weakest part of the training. I couldn't relax.

"The instructors ran a 'chase car' behind students doing the laps for a timed score. An instructor tailgated them to apply some pressure. I talked my way into riding shotgun with instructor Dick Barber. He talked me through his thinking, but more importantly I became acclimated to the speed, the g-forces, the 15% skid in corners. In the end, I had the fastest nighttime lap of anyone in my class.

"The 'receiving' language about the role of uke is not so much the role of punching bag for nage. Instead, the real 'receiving' that the role of uke offers is the deepest possible instruction. We become comfortable with the dynamics of a technique. We learn to surf its power in studying it many, many times 'from the inside'. This is why the best instructors all served as *uchi deshi* for some great instructor – starting of course with the first generation of shihan who served as uchi deshi to O-sensei.

"It is, however, a progression: we begin by wanting to 'receive' techniques without injury, then to service the training of the partner-nage by providing sincere attack and interaction, and finally we truly 'receive' a depth of understanding that can only come from studying techniques from within the storm. That last level is, of course, where we learn and develop *kaeshiwaza*.

"The way of uke is the most advanced level of study, in my opinion."

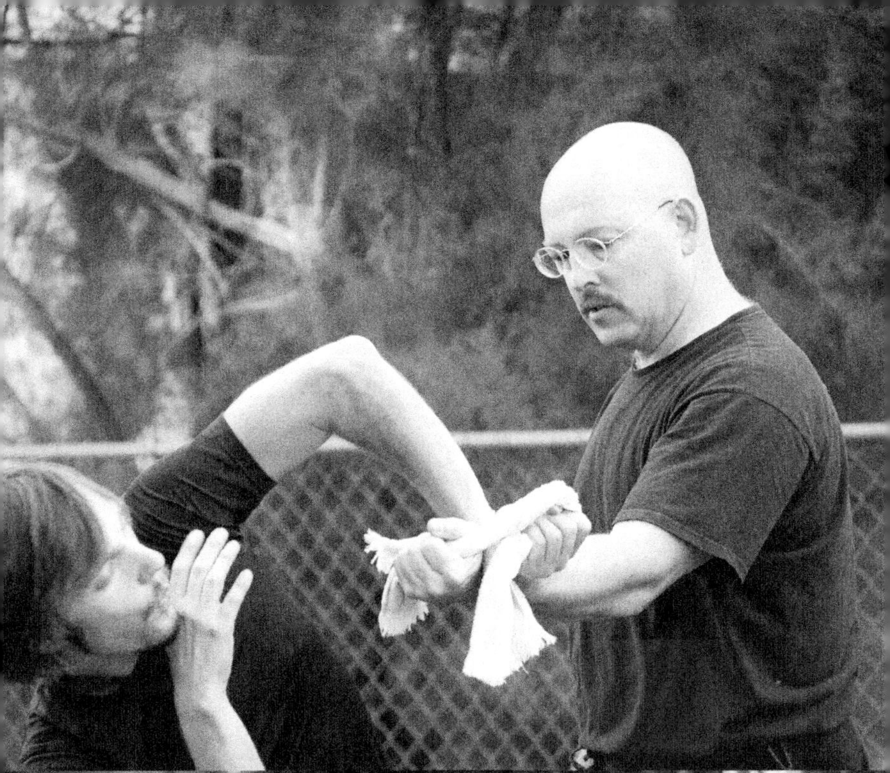
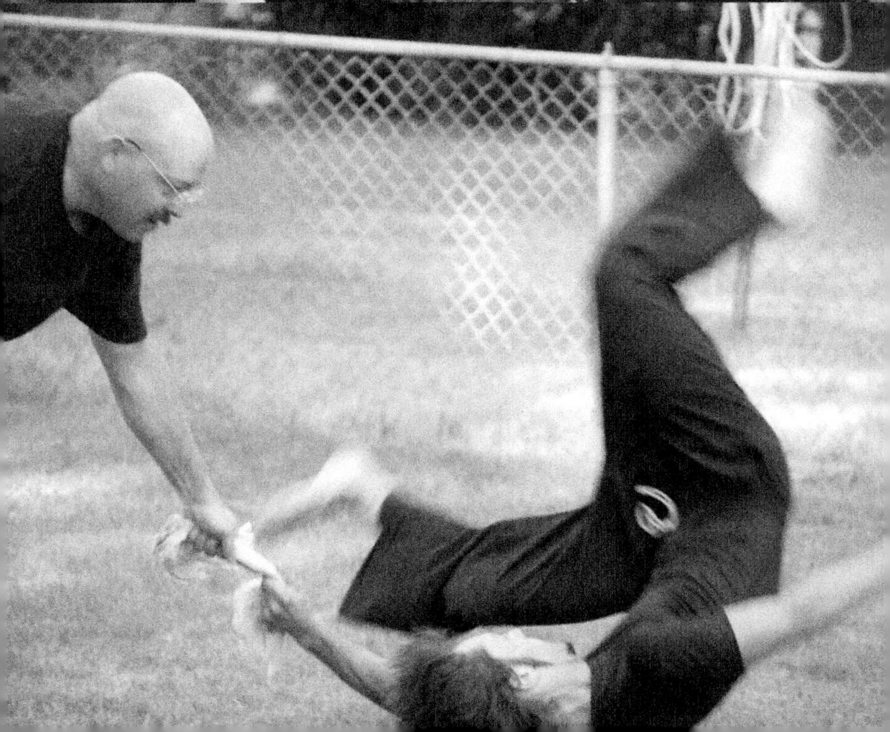

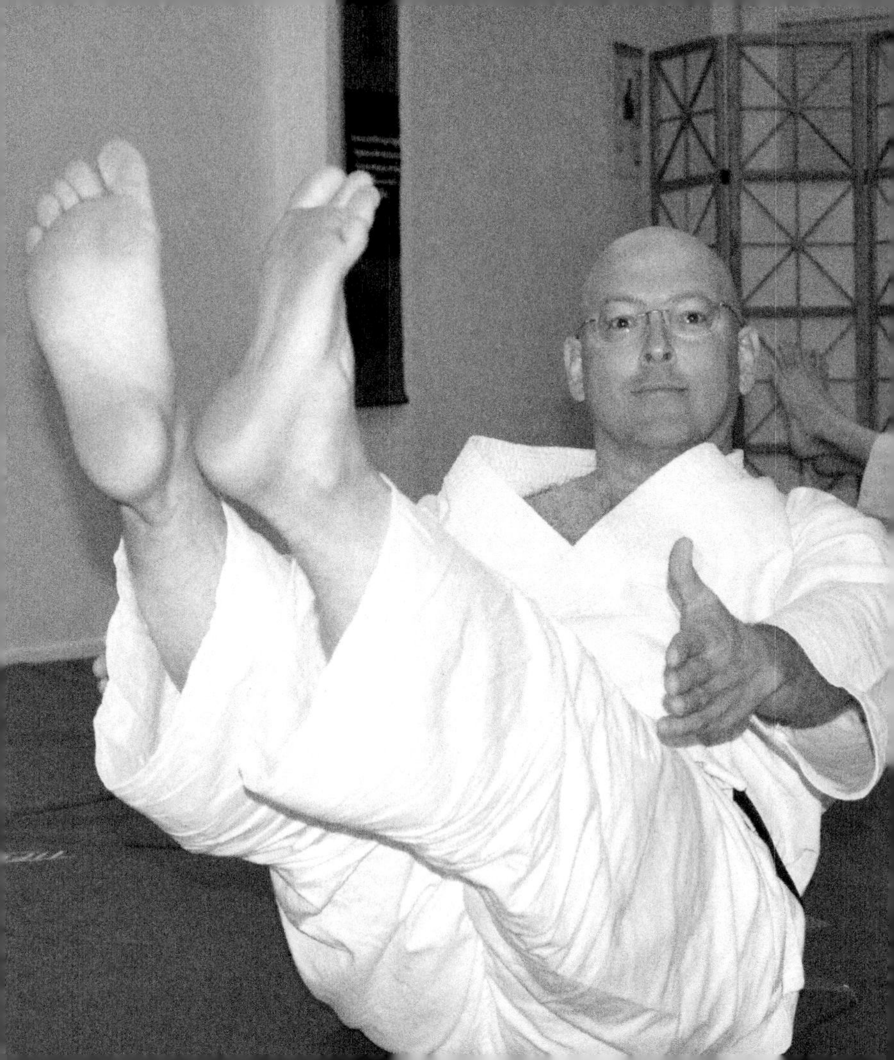

How to Develop an Aiki Body

"There is some discussion about how best to develop the 'Aiki body'. Some insist that Aikido already contains in itself all that is necessary to develop it. Others have pointed out that our standard practices and those of Morihei Ueshiba, who conceived Aikido, differ substantially, and that our curriculum should be supplemented accordingly. What do you think about this and what have you done and are you doing to help your Aiki body develop?"

"It's silly to pursue a goal that isn't well-defined. In the change-work field, we use the term 'well formed outcome'. It's a set of criteria or 'well-formedness conditions' to help ensure we don't set goals that aren't attainable, aren't within our control, aren't ecological, or maybe aren't even applicable to the actual needs. So, we might begin by asking 'What is an Aiki body?'

"It sounds like what many other systems call 'tool development' - to build the physical body to be suitable for the tasks involved in that art. And, we have to ask what that means to YOUR particular ideas. Are you a Navy SEAL? Are you a CIA assassin? Do you live in a high-violence, low-value-of-life part of the world? Are you an accountant in a small town in a country with an historically low rate of violence? What is your age – and your intention for longevity of practice?

"The answers to these things are unlikely to overlap with the answers O-sensei would give – at the different stages of his life – whether out in Hokkaido, on the 'Mongolian adventure', during the war, or even post-war. And, our modern, few-hours-per-week practices are not the same as O-sensei.

"For me, longevity in the art is a consideration – especially for the strong young macho bulls who will use up their bodies if not careful. I got good counselling on this from Tom Walker sensei when I thought I was bullet-proof. I managed only a couple of severe injuries over my career, and I'm mostly intact now. And, the more Aikido I practise the better everything functions.

"I practise – and recommend practising – a wide range of activities to build a well-rounded set of physical abilities and mental agility. I practise meditation, and Yoga. On occasion, I practise Iaido. I often do bag-work, on a standing bag, on a BOB bag, and on a head-band-mounted thing that smacks you in the eye if you miss it. I consistently do a variety of weight training regimens from traditional set-based days, HIIT training, and callisthenics like burpees - or Turkish get-ups. I hike, and climb mountains, and fly paragliders in a high thermal mountain environment. I still do some tactical firearms training once in a while. I obviously don't do every one of these things every day or even week. But, I do SOMETHING of it every day.

"My main advice is to do lots of things, to do them with consideration of your long-term fitness to function, and to think of applying Aikido principles where that's useful. Find activities that foster your goals and missions and do those.

"Limited kinds of movement and practice will result in a limited body and a limited way of thinking. Always be testing and reaching into something new. Keep the beginner's mind and body. It's really important to just keep

The Innovator

moving all the time. I set a timer during my days, working in 53-minute sprints punctuated by 7-minute activity periods to get blood flowing and work flexibility."

HIIT (High Intensity Interval Training) is a broad definition for training consisting of short periods of intense exercise intermixed with periods of recovery. An important plus of HIIT is that you can obtain maximum health benefits in a very limited amount of time.

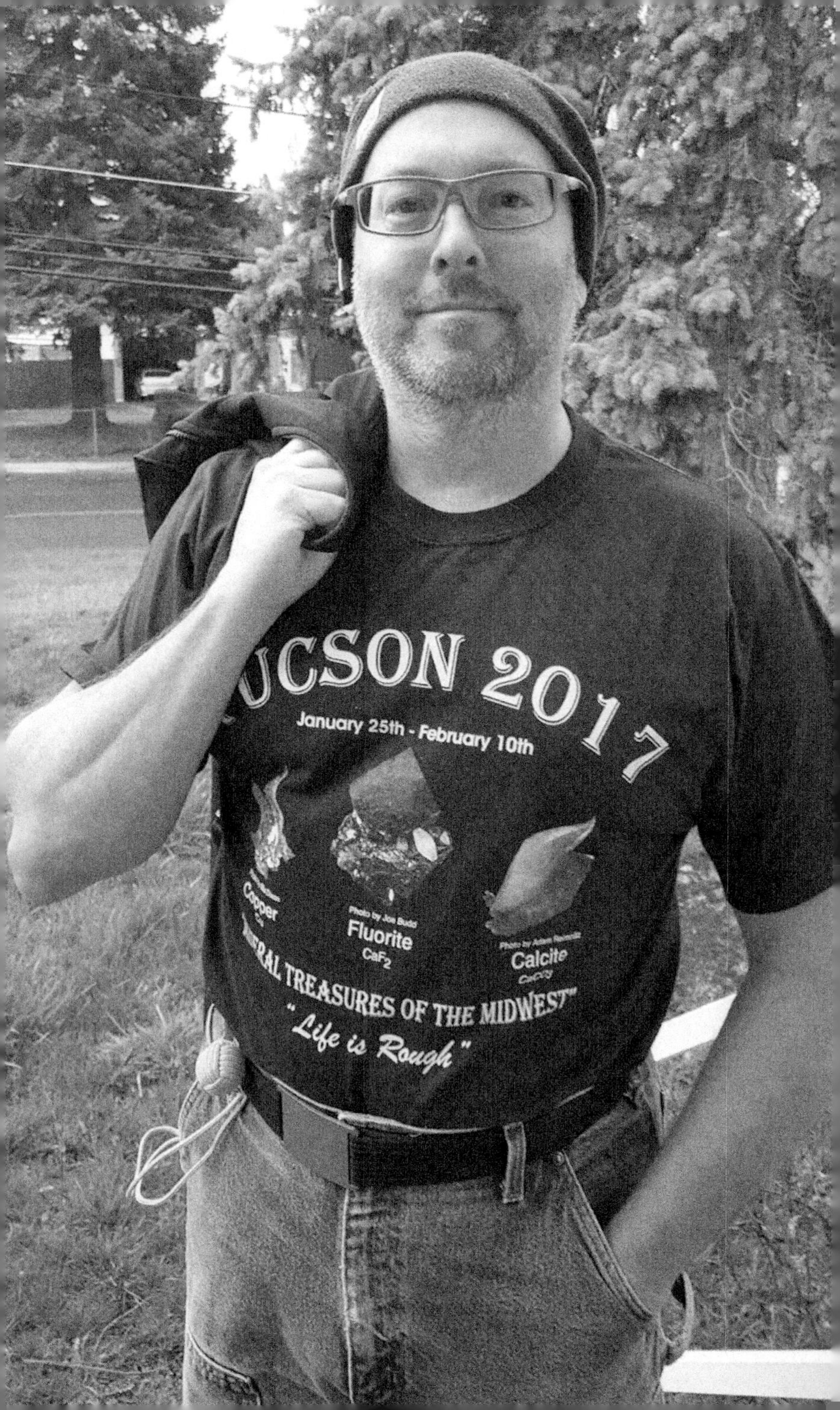

January 25th - February 10th
Copper
Fluorite
CaF2
Calcite
TREASURES OF THE MIDWEST"
" Life is Rough "

Is Cross Training a Bad Word?

"Many prominent pre-war Aikido figures were also specialists in Judo, Iaido or other branches of Budo. In more recent times, among the most famous and respected shihan, Shoji Nishio practised Karate, Judo and Iaido, while Yoshio Kuroiwa boxed. I am aware of the energy and time you have spent on cross-training and coming to terms with FMA. What would you say to those who accuse the innovators of our art of wanting to turn it into a kind of MMA in hakama and *aikidogi*? How do you handle the eternal dichotomy between tradition and innovation?"

"O-sensei was an original cross-trainer, wasn't he?
"There's a vast body of things O-sensei taught and trained that we don't see now – especially his pre-war material. I found that Aikido's tanto dori work is really weak compared to, e.g. Kali and Silat. And, I think some of the body work and body throws of Silat are just wonderful, fitting into Aikido movement seamlessly. My personal Aikido is pretty obviously contaminated with Kali, Silat and Karate.

"Functionally literate aikidoka will eventually all make Aikido their own to some extent – for their body, their age, their applications, especially if they do violence professionally.

"I once fought a demonstration match at a kickboxing event – because too many people got knocked out and they were running out of entertainment. I was still fighting tournament Karate, so when the host asked me, I said 'sure' and gloved-up. In Aikido, I was probably fourth – or possibly third kyu - at the time. They put me in the ring with a kickboxer kid that had arms a mile long, and he commenced beating me up.

"When he threw a body shot I avoided it with tenkan and trapped his glove under my elbow. Think classic *tsuki* kotegaeshi entrance, but no way to grab the wrist. I spun around and threw him across the ring into the ropes. He hated it, and the crowd literally booed me. But, I was grinning at 'Aikido in the kick-boxing ring'.

"So, I think body movement, and foundational principles are what make something Aikido or 'not Aikido'. I try not to judge harshly what others want in their Aikido. I try to stay focused on building what I want in mine, unless someone asks for my input or help. In that case, the first thing I do is ask them about their goals for their training. I try to facilitate whatever that is, because Aikido can be many good things for people. And, not everyone is any version of me.

"That said, I think cross-training is great, and Kali, Silat and Boxing are my top suggestions, paying special attention to how the techniques can integrate with the Aikido movement platform. Being in the States, I also recommend a familiarity and competence with firearms."

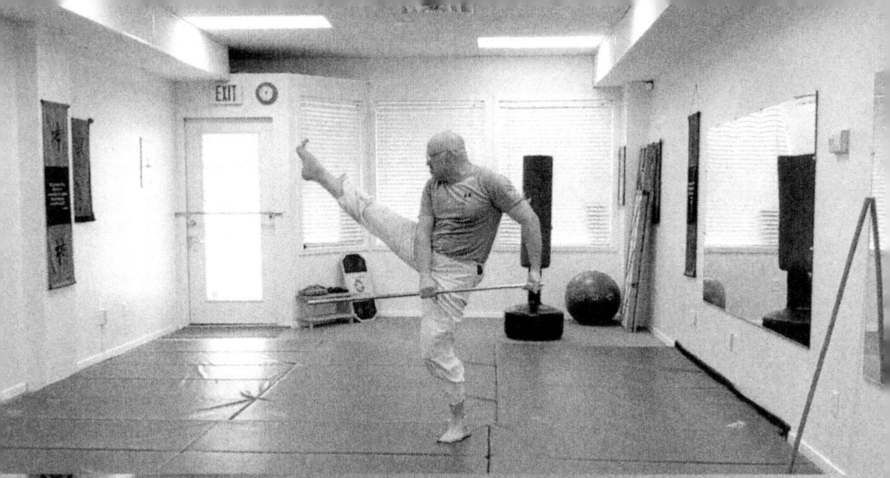
EXIT

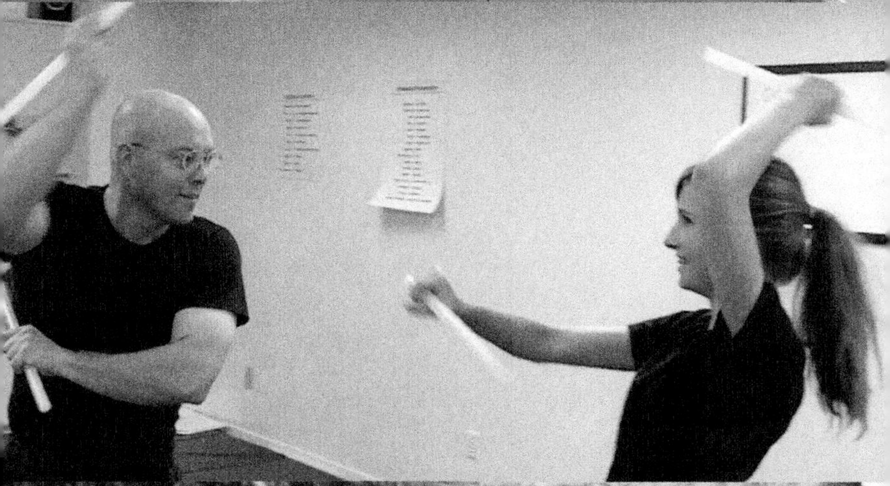

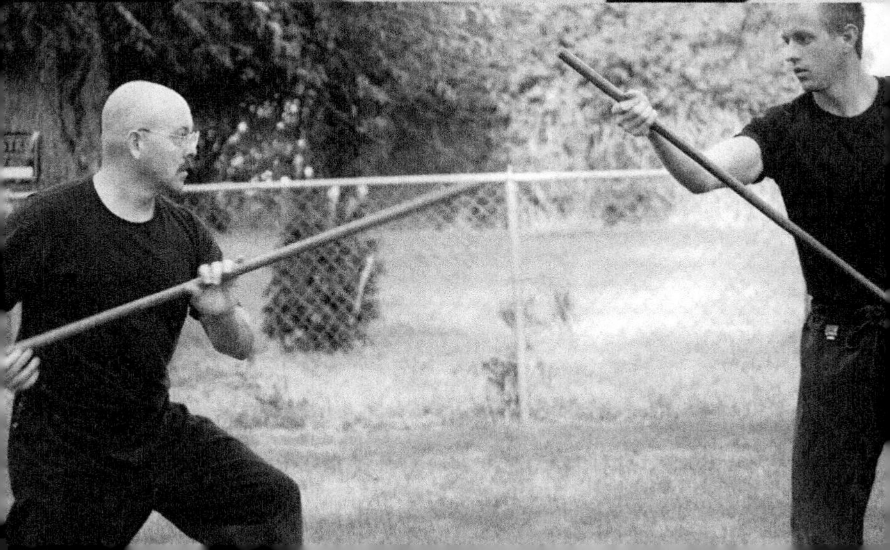

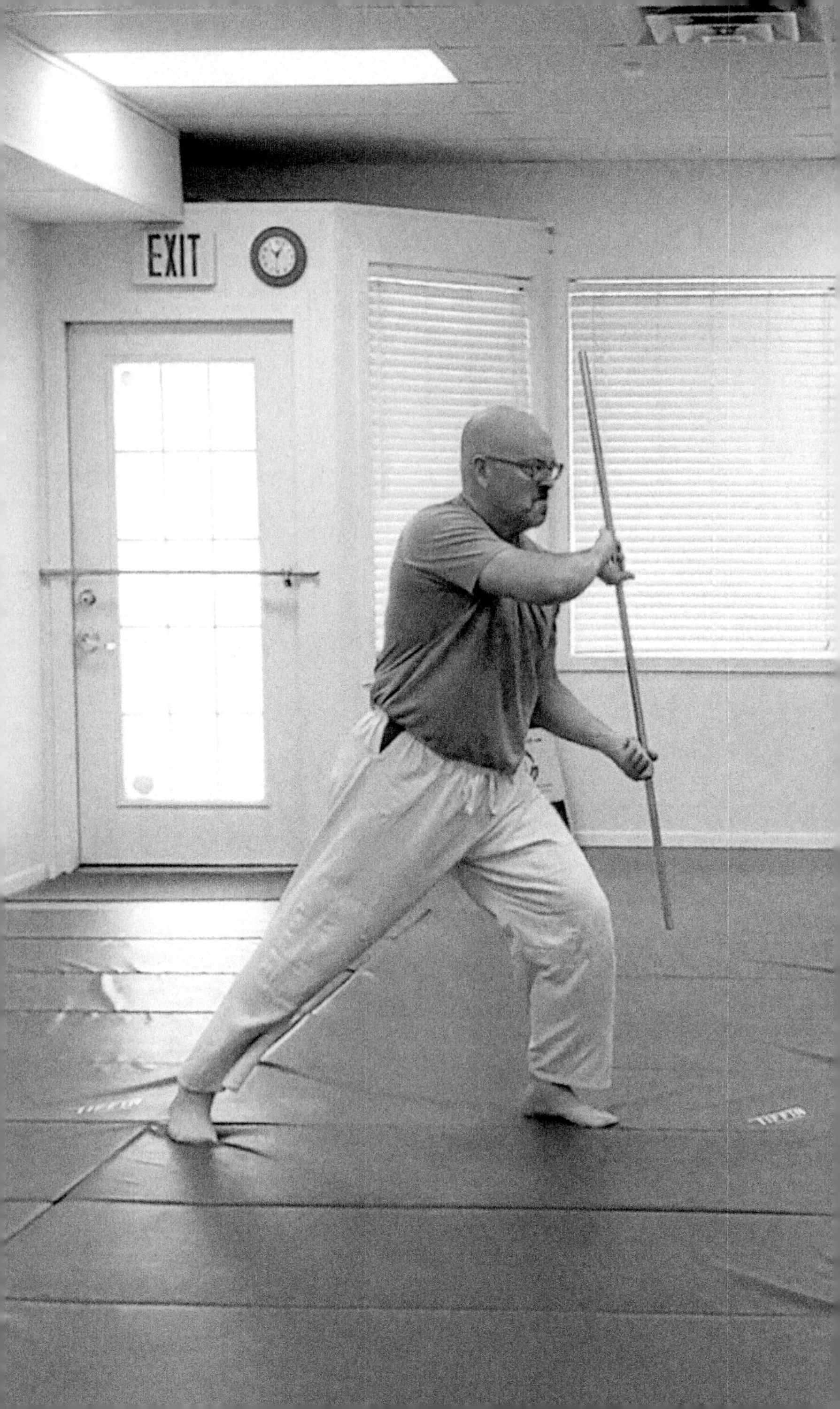
EXIT

To Compete or not To Compete?

"A couple of years ago, some Russian Aikikai groups experimented with a very light form of competition. It wasn't real sparring, or a direct confrontation between opponents, but some kind of kata-style demonstration with an award ceremony to follow. The Aikikai Foundation in the person of Mitsuteru Ueshiba sent them an official letter of reprimand, strongly declaring that competitions are forbidden in Aikido: 'It is the immutable will of the founder'.

"Today we do an infinite number of other things that would disgust Morihei Ueshiba, and this hardly seems to be a problem for anyone. We also tend to forget that competitions in Aikido have existed for a long time - not in Aikikai Aikido, but in other styles there are plenty of them, in different forms. It is not a mortal sin, it is simply considered a tool for training and growth, exactly as in other respectable Budo arts. What are your views on this extremely controversial topic?"

"I'm not a fan of turning martial things into games – whether tournament Karate or 'paper-punching' gun games – even though in the past I've fought tournament Karate and engaged in IPSC and other 'practical pistol' competitions. These things require great mental discipline to prevent them becoming both technical and ego problems.

"To me, anything martial is serious business, and should be done in that mindset and with tools and systems geared for that. It's not that a game-fighter isn't dangerous, it's that the practices can do more to reduce real tactical skills than to augment them. We become fixated on 'winning' in that context. The ego becomes a saboteur of quality training.

"So, my perspective is returning to my personal priorities and purposes for training in the first place. I think the kinds of Aikido demonstration-competition I've seen might promote flashy techniques to get points and might result in injuries from people excited to perform. I know even non-competitive public demonstrations can get people wound-up and result in injuries. I think Aikido is not for spectator entertainment.

"I don't condemn people who have different priorities. I just wouldn't be excited to participate myself in 'competitive Aikido', however one might structure it. The only person I'm interested in competing with is myself."

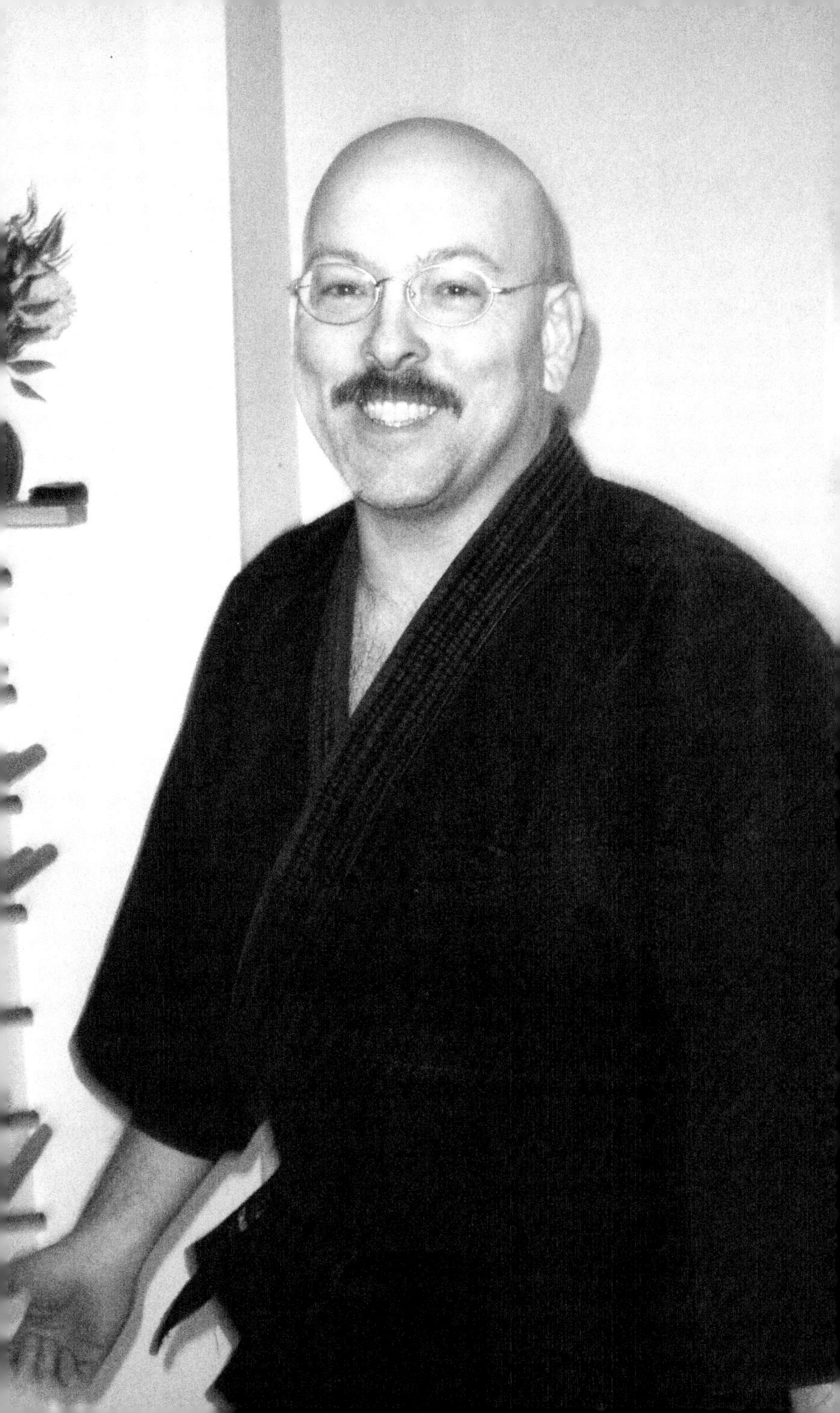

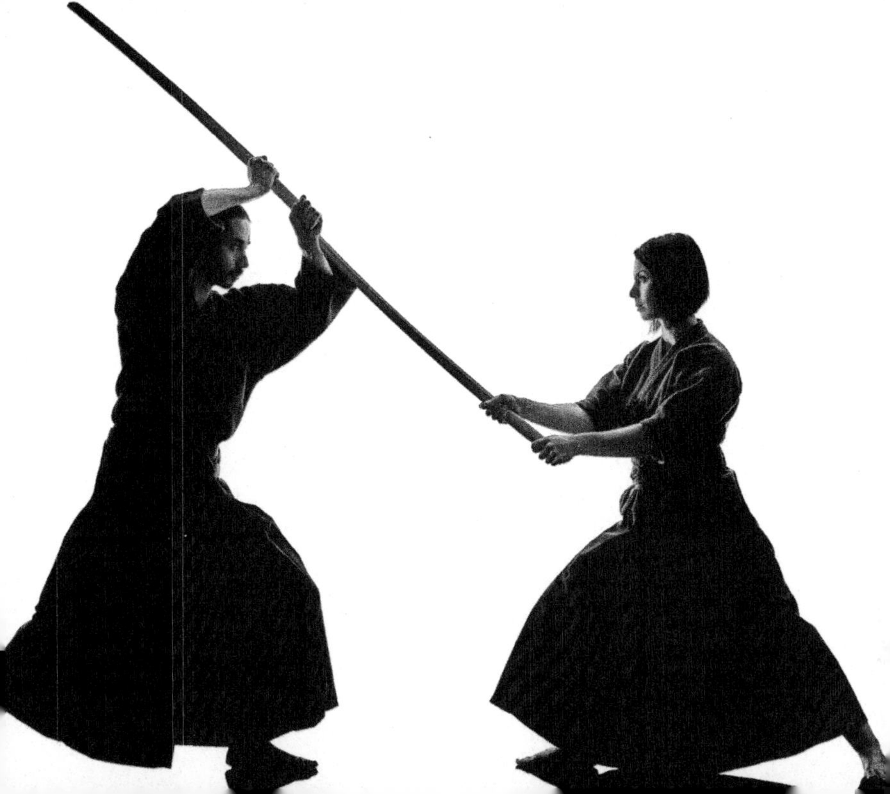

Supplement 1: Look Into the Mirror

In 2000, we released a thesis on progressive Aikido training methods. Within that work, we offered a concept dubbed "mirrors" or "mirrored techniques". This article is a short synopsis of that concept.

This is the entry from our current student manual referring to mirrors:

Mirror (mirrored entrance, movement, or technique):
Applies to an Entrance, Movement, Method or Technique that may be employed regardless of the side or lead from which the opponent launches aggression because the same movement will build a technique regardless of the "sidedness" or Matched/Unmatched lead of the attack. (syn: Symmetrical Entrance, Movement, or Technique). Mirrored Movements and Methods are generally taught and practised in pairs. This installs two techniques at once; makes use of twice the spatial references; and builds generalisation that speeds response time.

The concept sounds a bit odd at first, but studying with a partner will demonstrate its utility.
It is based on two premises:
1. O-sensei knew what he was about when he started

using movement to evade and confound attackers.

2. "A reasonable plan, violently executed immediately is better than a perfect plan,
ready next week." - Patton.

Here's a classic example:

1. We assume right hanmi, and Uke is also in right hanmi (matching lead), and we work from an attack with Uke's lead hand (In the US, this is sometimes called "New York style" attack), we'll interface ai-hand, ai-hanmi. We perform what most aikidoka would recognise as classical Ikkyo Ura. This is body-movement or foot-work that we call "taisabaki", moving to the outside of Uke's sphere of influence.

Our right hand attached at Uke's right wrist, and our left hand interfaced at or near Uke's elbow. We turned and cut downward.

2. We next maintain right hanmi, while Uke changes to left hanmi (unmatched lead), and
we'll again work from an attack with Uke's lead hand, to interface gyaku-hand, gyakuhanmi.

We perform the identical footwork, taking care to make atemi as we approach within range of Uke's free right hand. We enter deeply, taking Uke's balance, and attach at Uke's left wrist with our right hand, and with our left hand interfaced at Uke's left elbow (prepared position for one of Aikido's classical kokyunage methods). We cut down strongly, throwing Uke.

In the above example, we have practised a "perfect mirror" - a technique that allows identical movement irrespective of the lead from which Uke attacked.

The foot-work was identical; The interface was identical (wrist and elbow); and the completing cut can be identical (although the Ikkyo portion is smoother with an ura direction finish and the Kokyunage portion is smoother with a straight-line cut).

It is possible to use the identical foot-work, using Udekimenage for one termination and Sumiotoshi for the other. This is another "perfect mirror" combination.

After experimenting with this concept, it can be discovered that there are many "perfect" mirror combinations, and many that are not quite perfect - and that the concept applies to every standard entrance foot-work in Aikido.

For example, notice that ai-katatetori kotegaeshi (omote) is a very close mirror to gyaku-katatetori nikkyo (obi no sage version).

The existence of these relationships should not be a huge surprise, nor should they be discounted as an interesting point of trivia, as the training implications are substantial:

1. The need for knowing the sidedness of an attack is minimised if not negated. While an ai-hand attack opens kotegaeshi, a gyaku-hand attack opens nikkyo. The choice can be made after the initial threat has been evaded.

2. Every one movement has at least two applications, and may be practised from multiple stimuli - facilitating stronger generalisation of skills and reducing mental stalls under pressure.

3. Every entrance practised this way is as if practising two different entrances under the previous way of observing technique. This is more than a two-for-one discount because if techniques are practised in pairs, the constantly-shifting sidedness provides twice the spatial landmarks for the mind to utilise in locating "strong position". It in fact requires nage to be ever mindful of position in a more dynamic manner rather than a rote one where uke is simply expected to stay in

place.

4. Every terminating technique likewise provides a similar two-for-one discount, as well as a more extensive exploration of the relevant anatomical structures (rotating both clockwise and counter-clockwise in the Kotegaeshi-Nikkyo example).

More Reflections

Mirror-type practice may also be discovered when working against combination-type attacks, or follow-up attacks (more realistic attacks).

For instance, we can work a classical ai-hanmi jab-style attack, with taisabaki footwork (as above, like ikkyo ura form), but finish with kotegaeshi. This is very straightforward and quite common.

Change to gyaku-hanmi, and work the taisabaki movement against the jab - and we'll move
to Uke's "inside". We'll need atemi to keep Uke occupied, but he'll likely throw that cross behind the jab - either as a follow-up to our encroachment, or as the second half of a jab cross combination.
In either case, this affords us the opportunity to work with a more dynamic (and realistic) interaction with Uke, and as we deflect the second punch, we'll again acquire a kotegaeshi finish - on the hand that threw the cross.

So, with a single body movement and an almost identical hand placement, we can practice
kotegaeshi against the jab; we can practice nikkyo against the jab; and we can practice kotegaeshi (from the dangerous inside) against the jab-cross combination.

All that, USING THE SAME BODY MOVEMENT AND HAND PLACEMENT.

This is more than convenient, and more than interesting.

It's magical.

But, IT'S ONLY USEFUL IF PRACTISED TOGETHER with the specific goal of installing generalisation. The student must experience that these are not separate techniques or movements or methods, but that they are in fact ONE movement, with multiple, slightly varied final endings.

The student must experience this on a regular basis, as a matter of habitual presentation so the perception of "one method - many applications" becomes part of their understanding of Aikido – and therefore part of their application ability.

If not trained in a way that creates generalisation in the mind of the student, then the skill will not be available when needed.

How to Use Mirrors in Your Training (as instructor)

Whenever you decide to teach a technique, find that technique in the way you typically would, and perform it once.

Then, keeping your same hanmi, ask Uke to change to the opposite hanmi from his first attack - and perform/discover the mirror.

Doing this the first time is the only challenge. Once you've done it a few times, the oddness disappears and it becomes perfectly natural. You'll quickly find yourself automatically thinking in mirrored pairs of movements and techniques. When you daydream Aikido, you'll daydream it exploring these relationships and patterns.

Point out explicitly to students that we are not exploring two things, but different views of ONE THING. It is important they come to understand the technique as one thing, in order to maximise the benefit of this paradigm.

Make sure to demonstrate that Nage maintains RIGHT hanmi twice while Uke gives one attack from each hanmi so that Nage practises both the "inside" and the "outside" versions as ONE iteration.

Then, Nage changes to LEFT hanmi, and maintains it while Uke again offers both sides before the Nage/Uke roles change.

It is important that mirrors be practised in this fashion to install the generalisation the presentation was explicitly designed to create.

I recommend teaching any mirror-capable technique as a mirrored-pair whenever that presentation won't explicitly interfere with some other component of progression or presentation.

There are two other ways to use the mirror concept for teaching:

A. Work a method to the "outside" (e.g. classical tsuki-kotegaeshi). Then, change hanmi and use the same entrance to the (admittedly more dangerous) inside, working against a combination (e.g. jab-cross) attack. Terminate the interaction using the same technique - in this case, kotegaeshi - against Uke's back hand. This requires a very deep entrance, good timing, and atemi.

B. Work all three manifestations of the magic. Take the kotegaeshi example from (A) and add to it the obi-no-sage style nikkyo that can be applied against Uke's lead hand from the inside position (the direct mirror to the original kotegaeshi). Again, one needs a deep entrance, atemi, strong movement, but these are things we should be training, aren't they?

In all cases of using mirrors to train, the most important concept to remember is training
them together, presenting them as ONE thing rather than related or similar multiple things. The mind understands

ONE, and it will seize upon the opportunity to become more efficient.

The primary goals of mirrors training are:

1. Generalisation of a pattern, both in the direct physical realm - and in generalising Aikido throughout the rest of the student's life.

2. Increase efficiency of movement and of learning so every student may progress at an increasing rate of learning and an increasing level of fun.

Experimenting with mirrored pairs in a series of progressing techniques can be most instructive, yielding some fascinating things about related structures and methods. Explore for yourself.

How to Use Mirrors in Your Training
(as student)

First, follow your instructor's directions, and don't get off on a tangent in the corner. That's neither polite nor safe.

Provided your instructor doesn't object to this kind of practice, make an exercise of finding mirrors for various techniques. Whenever you see a technique demonstrated or on film, find the mirrors to discover what the reflection offers.

Remember that mirrors - especially perfect ones - are not different things, but different views of ONE THING. Think of them that way; Practice them that way.

You can also practise the "additional reflections" version by working against jab-cross and other related symmetrical combinations, discovering how deeply you must enter; what kind of atemi is required; how to bypass that second hand

Look into the Mirror

(whether it's coming high or low) - and to acquire the same terminating technique, regardless of those factors. This will go a long way toward allowing you to work dynamically.

When practising mirrors, remember that Nage practices twice from the same hanmi as Uke changes. Then, Nage changes and does the other pair. The point is for Nage to do the identical movement twice from the same physical position, but against different stimuli.

Only this pattern will install the generalisation that mirrors are designed to create.

When practising before or after class with classmates, train as above, and also search for mirrors of techniques you already know, noting relationships that are smooth and easy and ones that are not. You can't do anything "wrong" as long as you are careful and curious. The worst thing you'll do is find something that you will discover doesn't work well for you.

Along the way, you'll find many things that do.

Instructors and Students alike - whenever you want to see something new (or from a new perspective), just "look into the mirror".

Copyright © John Bailey
All rights reserved
Any unauthorised reproduction is strictly prohibited

Supplement 2: Cultural Conundrum

Every group that gathers will over time form a culture. This is not always - or even usually by careful design so much as by immediate practicality. It is then maintained by seniority, personality, and inertia. It's the story of the "electric monkeys":

> They put monkeys in a cage that was wired to shock them all viciously at the press of a button, and the button was pressed every time any one of them got close to a certain spot. The monkeys soon became violent toward anyone who approached that spot. Then, the wires were disconnected (no more shocks), and over time, monkeys were removed, one-by-one, and replaced by individuals who had never been shocked. But, entering the culture, they copied faithfully the cultural norm of attacking violently anyone who got near the "electric" spot. Eventually, there were no monkeys in the cage who had ever been shocked. Yet, they all still attacked anyone who got near the "electric" spot, because "that's the way things are done 'round here"...

Aikido was created by an individual who was creatively genius and socially unconventional.

Aikido was however created and built-up in the confines of the class-structured culture of compliance and conventionality and hierarchical rigidity of last century's Japan. Unfortunately for us, the culture of Aikido has since followed the cultural traditions of the country more than of the creative and unconventional proclivities of the man.

Cultural and linguistic inferences are orders of magnitude more powerful than words for creating a world-model. Any 5-year-old can point this out in the most elegant, if irreverent of ways, as children are wonderful detectors of discontinuity between actions and words (hypocrisies, in adult-speak).

Language creates and discloses culture - which is the consensual organisation of thoughts, ideas, and mores. For instance, use of the word "attack" presupposes a violent or evil intent. It implies certain things, and creates certain expectations, even if the thing being described was just a nasty or ignorant comment by a radio shock-jock.

Culture, including conventions of hierarchy, class, loyalty, etc. - form as ideas become practices and as those practices become the norm. In their original context, these kinds of things generally served some function - like keeping the whole group from getting shocked.

But, over time, "traditions" may lose their usefulness.

It has recently become acceptable in some Aikido circles to question the methods with which we train - perhaps even to question the goals of training. Many of my colleagues are talking about a "need for new methods" of training, and I certainly agree.

The challenge that I see with respect to this is that of cultural inertia. Like the electric monkeys, people harbour beliefs and habits and patterns of behaviour. Creativity is stifled by invisible boundaries deep in the mind before new ideas can be expressed.

Beliefs drive results. Individual belief-systems are interdependent with culture (communal belief-systems). Culture creates, installs, and maintains those communal beliefs through communications and rituals.

While training methods can be changed in the pursuit of better results, as long as the new methods are spawned from the same culture, they will be based in the same belief-systems that generated the old results - and the new results will be boringly-similar to what those same patterns created in the past.

New results can only be achieved by changing the culture, including the language and the supporting rituals of our Budo.

Taking Turns

When the roles of Uke and Nage are described in terms of "taking turns", it implies (to westerners, at least) that Uke is not just passive, but, literally "waiting their turn" to be an active participant. In the west, what is the typical mental and physical state of someone who is "waiting their turn"?

Instructing a beginner about "taking turns", infers to them that the role of Uke is like being at the bus stop or in the supermarket line: They can be told about "martial awareness" (unfamiliar crap), but they KNOW what "waiting your turn" means. And, most Aiki dojo culture presents (enforces, actually) Uke being a "passive" and waiting role.

Just as "taking turns" and culturally enforcing passivity on the part of Uke creates certain assumptions, beliefs - and results, other linguistic and cultural features of the typical Aiki dojo infer (install) certain beliefs, thereby setting in motion the forces that will ultimately create certain results.

Bowing

The habit of bowing habitually, reflexively, (neigh constantly) is another example. This is presented as a "showing of respect" - the word "respect" being the nearest polite translation of the concept, which would more accurately be translated as "fealty". It's as big a lie as claiming that "bowing to the tokonoma has no religious significance". (Last time I looked Shinto was considered a religion.)

In any case, one may easily find a modern culture within which immediate and reflexive performance of a "sign of respect" (to one's acknowledged superior) is compulsory: the Military.

The purpose of military salute is pretty obvious - as is the feudal Japanese cultural equivalent.
Both rituals have very similar structural origins - feudal / military societies rife with caste-like class structure.

You can talk it all you like, call it what you like, and rationalise it. Translate it into Swahili if you want. The culture of actions remains more powerful than words at creating a world-view on deep cognitive levels.

In bowing, we have a behaviour based in a feudal military and social system that ritualised gestures of fealty and submission. My question is about our goals, both for students and for ourselves:

1. Maximise human potential through fostering individual growth, leadership, and self-actualisation; or 2. Insure compliance, submissiveness, deference, fealty. Or maybe, feel really superior because everyone around is constantly groveling in support of the delusion.

Which is it?

A person can try denial, or plead innocent by reason of rationalisation. They can try a cover-up of words. They can even claim temporary Dungeons and Dragons (aka dress-up and play Japanese). But, no one can escape the consequences of systematically-imposed rituals of submission and status. And, consequences to the instructor's ego are even more insidious than those to the student…

Some have responded to my first draft of this material by asserting that the ritualised actions do not have the same effect if one thinks they believe something else - or if one is not "living in the culture". Of course, if someone is engaging in the ritual of the culture then they are subject to the ritual's effects – intended or not. Some of those responses have been quite emotional…

The purpose of ritual is to install and maintain a belief-system (culture). The power of ritual is that conscious thought is not required for the ritual to do that. In fact, NOT thinking about the ritual is part of what helps to install it to the unconscious level of belief - the level from which unreasoned emotional response always arises when the light of reason or science fall upon dogma.

So, my answer to those who are "offended" by my observations, or who experience powerful emotional response - is QED: Congratulations: You are a very good hypnotic subject.

Honorifics

This issue is similar to bowing. There are the three S's: Shihan, Shidoin, and Sensei - followed by Uchi-Deshi, Sempai, Kohai, and others - all of which, because of their origin in a class-based culture, serve to perpetuate those same cultural divisions (and divisiveness), even now.

Again, I question the usefulness of this in our context and for our stated purposes. We are not soldiers and our culture is not feudal. We are an open society that is ostensibly free from class stricture and within which everyone is ostensibly free to rise to the level of the competence their tenacity will support. Even in the largest dojo, we do not need a fancy title to know who collects fees, pays the rent, leads the class, and locks the door.

Either it's just "cool" to have these titles - I'm flashing back to Dungeons and Dragons again - or, maybe it's "cool" to have people calling me "Sensei" (and expecting me to bestow the wisdom of the Buddha), or perhaps it is all part of the "electric monkey syndrome" and this silliness has long outlasted any objective utility…

This problem extends into every corner of our art, all the way from these questionable rituals, to the disorganisation of techniques, to the use of vague and dated colloquial Japanese terms that aren't descriptive enough to be standardised across political bodies or to allow even very experienced veterans of the art communicate concisely about technical issues.

It's time to evaluate the changes our art needs, starting by designing our desired results. That includes defining who we want to teach; what we want to teach them; and whether they will happily pay to learn that in the context we offer it. Maybe we'll be a little curious about the student's goals?

The second step is to design, deliberately, and with careful thought, the culture that will support our outcome. We must also deliberately and purposefully design the rituals that will create and support that culture both in our context and over time. We should build-in protections against the kind of cultural stagnation and dogmatic behaviours and class stricture that has led us far from the founder's unique personal pattern of innovation and integration.

Culture drives results, regardless of the methods one chooses, because culture, as the collective belief-system, defines perception; sets criteria; and most significantly, it constrains creativity in generating new methods. Therefore, changing the underlying (limiting) culture is prerequisite to discovering and implementing changes of methods that can generate substantively different results.

Only after creating a new culture will be we prepared to design, test, and implement the specific training methodologies that will produce a truly new result. Only by breaking-free from the feudal culture of fealty as maintained by clinging to no-longer-useful rituals of that feudal time, will we permit ourselves the creativity to allow our Budo to live and breathe anew.

I personally think people should get their religion at home; that in 21st Century America, we should speak English; that Bruce Lee was right when he said "Martial arts are the sincerest form of self-expression" - and that our culture should facilitate creativity and expression more than it should impose conformity - especially artificial, outdated, foreign, class-structure-based conformity.

Lastly, I believe that if you want to get my attention on the street or in the dojo, you should use the name my mother gave me for that very purpose.

Copyright © John Bailey
All rights reserved
Any unauthorised reproduction is strictly prohibited

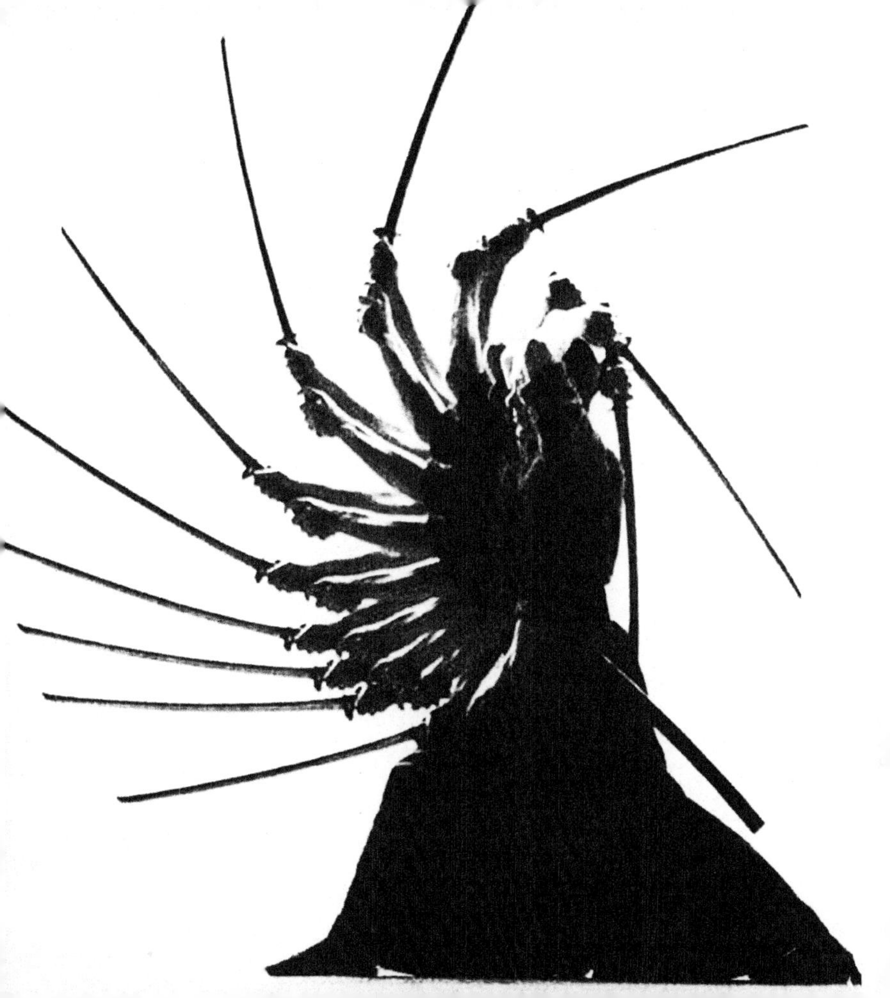

The Aiki Dialogues

1. The Phenomenologist - Interview with Ellis Amdur
2. The Translator - Interview with Christopher Li
3. The Wrestler - Interview with Rionne "Fujiwara" McAvoy
4. The Traveler - "Find Your Way" - Interview with William T. Gillespie
5. Inryoku - "The Attractive Force" - Interview with Gérard Blaize
6. The Philosopher - Interview with André Cognard
7. The Hermeticist - Interview with Paolo N. Corallini
8. The Heir - Interview with Hiroo Mochizuki
9. The Parent - Interview with Simone Chierchini
10. The Sensei - About Yoji Fujimoto
11. The Teacher - Interview with Lia Suzuki
12. The Innovator: Interview with John Bailey

Simone Chierchini: The Phenomenologist
Interview with Ellis Amdur
The Aiki Dialogues - N. 1

Ellis Amdur is a renowned martial arts researcher, a teacher in two different surviving Koryū and a former Aikidō enthusiast.
His books on Aikidō and Budō are considered unique in that he uses his own experiences, often hair-raising or outrageous, as illustrations of the principles about which he writes. His opinions are also backed by solid research and boots-on-the-ground experience.
"The Phenomenologist" is no exception to that.

Simone Chierchini: The Translator - Interview with Christopher Li
The Aiki Dialogues - N. 2

Christopher Li is an instructor at the Aikido Sangenkai, a non-profit Aikidō group in Honolulu, Hawaii, on the island of Oahu. He has been training in traditional and modern Japanese martial arts since 1981, with more than twelve years of training while living in Japan. Chris calls himself a "hobbyist with a specialty", however, thanks to his research and writing he has made an important contribution to the understanding of modern Aikidō. His views on Aikidō, its history and future development are unconventional and often "politically incorrect" but he's not afraid to share them. This is not a book for those unwilling to discuss the official narrative of our art and its people.

Simone Chierchini: The Wrestler - Interview with Rionne McAvoy
The Aiki Dialogues - N. 3

From Taekwondo wonder kid to Karate State Champion, from Hiroshi Tada Sensei's Gessoji Dojo to the Aikikai Hombu Dojo and Yoshiaki Yokota sensei, Rionne "Fujiwara" McAvoy, a star in the toughest professional wrestling league in the world, Japan, has never been one for finding the easy way out. In "The Wrestler", Rionne McAvoy tells his story in martial arts and explains his strong views on Aikido, physical training and cross-training and reveals where he wants to go with his Aikido.

Simone Chierchini: The Traveler - Find Your Way
Interview with William T. Gillespie
The Aiki Dialogues - N. 4

William T. Gillespie, the author of the book "Aikido in Japan and The Way Less Traveled", is a pioneer of Aikido in China. As the sign in his first Aikido Dojo in Los Angeles read, "Not even a million dollars can buy back one minute of your life". This is why W.T. Gillespie resigned from a professional career as a trial attorney in Los Angeles, to move to Tokyo to devote himself to intensively study Aikido at the Aikikai World Headquarters. Currently a 6th Dan Aikikai, his martial arts adventures in Japan and beyond to South East Asia, Korea and even The People's Republic of China became a fantastic journey of self-discovery and personal development that continues to unfold.

Simone Chierchini: Inryoku
The Attractive Force
Interview with Gérard Blaize
The Aiki Dialogues - N. 5

Gérard Blaize, the first non-Japanese Aikido expert to receive the rank of 7th dan Aikikai, spent five and a half years in Japan where he studied Aikido at the Hombu Dōjō in Tōkyō. In 1975, he met Michio Hikitsuchi, one of the most respected personal students of the founder of Aikido Morihei Ueshiba, and followed his sole guidance until his teacher's death in 2004. Hikitsuchi Sensei was a Shinto priest as well as a high ranked martial artist; in 1969 he was personally awarded the 10th Dan rank by O-sensei. Gérard Blaize has inherited and is still carrying the legacy of Hikitsuchi's holistic Aikido to this day.

Simone Chierchini: The Philosopher
Interview with André Cognard
The Aiki Dialogues - N. 6

André Cognard is one of the most authoritative voices in contemporary international Budo. Born in 1954 in France, he approached the world of martial arts at a very young age, dedicating himself to the intensive practice of various traditional Japanese disciplines. In 1973 he met Hirokazu Kobayashi sensei, a direct disciple of O-sensei Morihei Ueshiba. He received the rank of 8th Dan and on the death of his mentor inherited the leadership of the academy Kokusai Aikido Kenshukai Kobayashi Hirokazu Ryu. An "itinerant" teacher, a profound connoisseur of Japan and its traditions, André Cognard brings worldwide a technique – the Aikido of his Master; a human message – Aikido at the service of all; a spiritual message – Aikido which, like Man, reconnects with itself when it simply becomes Art.

**Simone Chierchini: The Hermeticist
Interview with Paolo N. Corallini**
The Aiki Dialogues - N. 7

Paolo N. Corallini has been practicing the Art of Aikido since 1969 and during his career he has held numerous positions in this art at national and international level. Author of many conferences on Aikido and its Spirituality, he has written 6 volumes on this martial art. A scholar of Eastern philosophies and religions such as Taoism, Shintoism, Esoteric Buddhism and Sufism, he loves the world of chivalric tradition in general and the Knights Templar in particular. In "The Hermeticist" Corallini sensei brings the reader from Iwama and his meeting with Morihiro Saito sensei to the complex interweaving between the different pedagogies in Aikido; from his memories of the man Morihiro Saito to the future of Aikido and much much more.

**Adriano Amari: The Heir
Interview with Hiroo Mochizuki**
The Aiki Dialogues - N. 8

Hiroo Mochizuki is the heir of a samurai family. Creator of Yoseikan Budo, he is a world-renowned expert in Japanese martial arts.
Son of the famous teacher Minoru Mochizuki, who is considered a Japanese national treasure and was also a direct student of Jigoro Kano and Morihei Ueshiba, the successor of a line of samurai, Hiroo Mochizuki was inspired by his forefathers combative spirit to create Yoseikan Budo.
He adapted the philosophy, pedagogy and traditional practice of martial arts to a new modern environment, as well as to contemporary combat techniques. Besides practicing Mixed Martial Arts before people knew what MMA was, Hiroo Mochizuki has one of the most impressive records in the martial world.

Marco Rubatto: The Parent
Interview with Simone Chierchini
The Aiki Dialogues - N. 9

Simone Chierchini did not choose Budo, he "was there". For 50 years at the forefront and in an enviable position in the Aikido community, he had the opportunity to witness first-hand the major events that have accompanied the birth and development of Aikido in Italy and Europe. Simone began practicing Aikido at the age of eight and has travelled the world as a student and teacher of the art, changing friends, students and occupations but never forgetting to pack his sword, pen and camera. A direct pupil of Hideki Hosokawa and Yoji Fujimoto, Simone has recently founded Aikido Italia Network Publishing, the publishing house specialised in the dissemination of Aikidō and martial arts culture that hosts this interview.

Simone Chierchini: The Sensei
About Yoji Fujimoto
The Aiki Dialogues - N. 10

This publication endeavours to accomplish a very difficult task: that of bringing to life once again the voice and works of one of the most beloved figures of International Aikidō. Yoji Fujimoto sensei has been gone for nearly 10 years and has left behind thousands of students who have who have never stopped mourning him. Since 1971, the year of his arrival in Italy, Fujimoto sensei has dedicated his whole life and all his energy to the practice of Aikidō. In this book, some of Fujimoto sensei's senior students have tried, within the limits of their abilities and their memories, to evoke the figure and teaching of Fujimoto sensei.

**Simone Chierchini: The Teacher
Interview with Lia Suzuki**
The Aiki Dialogues - N. 11

Lia Suzuki, founder and director of Aikido Kenkyukai International USA, began her Aikido training in 1982 under William Gleason. She soon moved to Japan to train with Yoshinobu Takeda, one of Seigo Yamaguchi's most accomplished students. She lived in Japan and trained extensively in Aikido from 1987 to 1996. At the urging of Takeda shihan, Lia sensei returned to establish dojos in the USA in 1996. She currently holds the rank of 6th dan Aikikai and travels extensively as a guest instructor, conducting Aikido seminars in dojos around the world. Over the years, Lia sensei has dedicated her training to promoting inclusion in the world of Aikido and increasing the popularity of Aikido among young people.

NEXT ISSUE:

The Aiki Dialogues N°13

Simone Chierchini

The Uchideshi

Interview with
Jacques Payet

Jacques Payet has been a student of Aikido since 1980, when he first moved to Japan to learn under one the Aikido greatest, Gozo Shioda.
It was during this time that he became the longest serving foreign uchideshi to serve at the Yoshinkan.
In the Yoshinkan organization he achieved the rank of Hachidan (8th dan) and the title of Shihan.
Today Payet sensei is the Head Instructor of the Mugenjuku, his own dojo based in Kyoto, Japan. He is also the creator of a well-known Senshusei course, the translator of several important Aikido works and an author himself.
In this book we retrace the rich martial path that led him from Shioda sensei to us: a human adventure, a daily challenge, physical and mental, a unique training that has shaped him for ever.

Printed in Great Britain
by Amazon